Child Abuse

by Bonnie Juettner

LUCENT BOOKS

A part of Gale, Cengage Learning

Detroit • New York • San Francisco • New Haven, Conn • Waterville, Maine • London

© 2009 Gale, Cengage Learning

LIBRARY OF CONGRESS CATALOGING-IN-PUBLICATION DATA

Juettner, Bonnie.
  Child abuse / by Bonnie Juettner.
    p. cm. — (Hot topics)
  Includes bibliographical references and index.
  ISBN 978-1-4205-0118-6 (hardcover)
  1. Child abuse—United States—Juvenile literature. 2. Abused children—United States—Juvenile literature. I. Title.
  HV6626.52.J84 2009
  362.760973—dc22

                                        2008052818

Lucent Books
27500 Drake Rd.
Farmington Hills, MI 48331

ISBN-13: 978-1-4205-0118-6
ISBN-10: 1-4205-0118-6

Printed in the United States of America
1 2 3 4 5 6 7 13 12 11 10 09

CONTENTS

FOREWORD

Young people today are bombarded with information. Aside from traditional sources such as newspapers, television, and the radio, they are inundated with a nearly continuous stream of data from electronic media. They send and receive e-mails and instant messages, read and write online "blogs," participate in chat rooms and forums, and surf the Web for hours. This trend is likely to continue. As Patricia Senn Breivik, the former dean of university libraries at Wayne State University in Detroit, has stated, "Information overload will only increase in the future. By 2020, for example, the available body of information is expected to double every 73 days! How will these students find the information they need in this coming tidal wave of information?"

Ironically, this overabundance of information can actually impede efforts to understand complex issues. Whether the topic is abortion, the death penalty, gay rights, or obesity, the deluge of fact and opinion that floods the print and electronic media is overwhelming. The news media report the results of polls and studies that contradict one another. Cable news shows, talk radio programs, and newspaper editorials promote narrow viewpoints and omit facts that challenge their own political biases. The World Wide Web is an electronic minefield where legitimate scholars compete with the postings of ordinary citizens who may or may not be well-informed or capable of reasoned argument. At times, strongly worded testimonials and opinion pieces both in print and electronic media are presented as factual accounts.

Conflicting quotes and statistics can confuse even the most diligent researchers. A good example of this is the question of whether or not the death penalty deters crime. For instance, one study found that murders decreased by nearly one-third when the death penalty was reinstated in New York in 1995. Death penalty supporters cite this finding to support their argument that the existence of the death penalty deters criminals from committing murder. However, another study found that states without the death penalty have murder rates below the national average. This study is cited by opponents of capital punishment, who reject the claim that the death penalty deters murder. Students need context and clear, informed discussion if they are to think critically and make informed decisions.

The Hot Topics series is designed to help young people wade through the glut of fact, opinion, and rhetoric so that they can think critically about controversial issues. Only by reading and thinking critically will they be able to formulate a viewpoint that is not simply the parroted views of others. Each volume of the series focuses on one of today's most pressing social issues and provides a balanced overview of the topic. Carefully crafted narrative, fully documented primary and secondary source quotes, informative sidebars, and study questions all provide excellent starting points for research and discussion. Full-color photographs and charts enhance all volumes in the series. With its many useful features, the Hot Topics series is a valuable resource for young people struggling to understand the pressing issues of the modern era.

INTRODUCTION

MORE THAN A MILLION CHILDREN

home (hōm) *n.* **1.** A place where one lives; a residence. **2.** The physical structure within which one lives, such as a house or apartment. **3.** A dwelling place together with the family or social unit that occupies it; a household. **4a.** An environment offering security and happiness. **b.** A valued place regarded as a refuge.[1]

For most American children, home is more than a place to live. It is a place to be safe, secure, and happy—a place where they can always expect to be taken care of. It is a place where family members are happy for them when they have a good day and comfort them when they experience hard times. Home is a refuge.

But for more than a million children every year, home is anything but a refuge. Some children—in the United States, more than 573,000 in 2005—live in homes where their needs are not met. Their homes do not always have food in the refrigerator. They may not have adequate clothes to wear. Their parents do not take them to the doctor when they need health care. These children are neglected.

Other children—more than 230,000 in 2005—cannot trust their families or caretakers to be kind to them. Sometimes, their family members physically hurt them. The list of things that happen to these children is heartbreaking to read. Adults may hit them, burn them, slam fingers in doors, expose them to dangerous chemicals, or sexually abuse them. Some adults try to hurt children by forcing them to stay outside for hours in severely cold weather without shoes or a coat. They may interrupt their sleep or try to scare a child by driving recklessly. Some adults have attacked children with weapons such as guns or knives.

Younger children are even more likely to be abused than older kids. Some adults become so frustrated with a baby's cries that they shake the baby until it has brain damage or until it dies. At other times, adults react to the normal behavior of toddlers and preschoolers by beating them. Sometimes they tie children up or put them in cages.

Physical abuse and neglect can occur simultaneously. In August 2008 state troopers in Michigan pulled over a car. In it they found a four-week-old baby and his teenage parents. The baby was not in a car seat. The lack of a car seat was considered neglect. The baby also had a pacifier taped to his mouth. This was physical abuse. In this case the troopers arranged for the baby to be temporarily placed in the custody of his grandparents. Meanwhile, the Michigan Department of Human Services provided parenting classes to help the teenagers learn how to care for a baby.

Many children—more than 208,000 in 2005—are abused not just physically, but psychologically as well. Their parents threaten them or belittle them with verbal put-downs. They may constantly call a child dumb or stupid or make fun of a child's appearance. Or they may find ways to humiliate a child. For example, a fifteen-year-old living in Anchorage, Alaska, told an interviewer that when she was in fourth grade, her mother started coming to her school drunk. Her mother would pull her out of class and scream at her and at her teachers in front of her classmates. This type of abuse, emotional abuse, is sometimes called the "invisible child abuse."

Physical abuse and emotional abuse are not always separate. Physical abuse does cause emotional, as well as physical, injuries. However, social workers also investigate some cases in which children are abused emotionally but not physically.

Even at times when no one is hurting them, abused children cannot feel safe. They live with the fear that something they do or do not do may trigger an act of abuse, or that a caregiver may have a bad day and come home in a bad mood, or that this may be the day when a parent drinks too much or takes drugs. At home, they may feel as though anything could happen at any time. They try hard to behave in ways that will not lead to abuse. They may or may not realize that children do not cause abuse—adults do. An abusive adult will lash out for his or her own reasons—no matter what a child does or does not do.

For these children, even sleeping may offer no relief. Richard Pelzer, a man who has written about the abuse he experienced as a youth, writes: "I had perfected the ability to sleep with my eyes open and be aware of any movement within my line of vision. It was an alarm system I used when I slept. Often as a child, I was able to bring myself back into consciousness if I saw Mom cross my line of vision as she walked into my room at night. It was a safety mechanism."[2]

Pelzer's story has a happy ending. When he was a teenager, his family moved. He met neighbors he grew to trust. He told them his story. Concerned, they did some research for him and found a foster home program that accepted teenagers. Pelzer registered himself in the program. Later, as an adult himself, he began writing books to help raise awareness about child abuse.

Children who are victims of abuse feel trapped in their circumstances.

For some child abuse victims, there is no happy ending. In 2005 child abuse and neglect caused 1,460 deaths in the United States. For the survivors, though, the story does not end with the abuse. Each story continues in its own way. Some children live with the abuse until they are old enough to leave home. Some tell an adult they trust—and the trusted adult gets help for the child. Others tell an adult, but the adult does not believe them, and the abuse continues. Some become part of a child welfare investigation. In most cases, the state offers resources to the families to help them care for their children. But some children are taken from their homes and enter foster care. Some of these children are cared for by a relative, such as a grandparent. Others go to live with foster parents who are not related to them. Still others run away from home or are legally emancipated by a court.

Each survivor of abuse must travel his or her own path toward healing. First the abuse has to stop. Once the abuse stops for good, survivors can begin to heal. First they heal from their physical injuries. Eventually, emotional healing begins as well. Given time, survivors can recover.

How Serious Is Child Abuse in the United States?

When security expert Gavin de Becker was a child, he lived in Los Angeles with his physically abusive mother. One night, de Becker feared for his sister's safety. He tried to stop his mother from beating her. As he intervened, his sister ran out the door into the street. De Becker followed. He writes:

> We stopped at an all-night market and decided to make an anonymous call to the police ("There are two kids loitering around here"). If we didn't give our names to the police, we concluded, they wouldn't be able to take us back home. And it worked just like that. Our ride from the LAPD showed up within a few minutes and took us to jail. They could hardly put a twelve-year-old boy and a fourteen-year-old girl in with hardened criminals (though we might have felt at home), so they put us in our own cell. In the morning, we called our grandfather, who picked us up and took us home. Two kids found bruised and red-eyed and panting at three-thirty in the morning, and nobody asked us a thing. It was as if the police saw these dramas every day, and I know now that they do.[3]

How Widespread Is Child Abuse?

When he grew up, de Becker found out how common child abuse is. Now he works with organizations and families to prevent child abuse. As children, however, he and his sister thought their home life was normal. Many abuse survivors feel the same way, until they have a chance to observe friends whose homes are quite different. Until then, they assume all families are like theirs.

It is difficult for experts to determine how many cases of child abuse occur in the United States every year. Also, government statistics on child abuse are always two or three years out of date, because the statistics are carefully reviewed before they are released to the public. In 2005 more than 3 million cases of suspected child abuse or neglect were reported to the authorities. This means that about 3 million times, someone called child welfare authorities to report that children were in danger. The number of children in danger, though, is greater than the number of calls. Usually, each call is connected with one family, which may have more than one child. In 2005 the 3 million calls concerned more than 6 million children. The person making the

A Kansas state trooper walks by cutouts laid on the steps of the state courthouse to represent the victims of child abuse.

call may be a child's relative, friend, or neighbor, or even a concerned stranger. Or it might be a mandated reporter—someone who is required by law to report suspected cases of child abuse. Teachers, doctors, nurses, police officers, and social workers are all mandated reporters. So are members of the clergy.

Not every phone call represents a genuine case of abuse. Of the 3 million initial phone calls reporting abuse in the United States in 2005, child welfare investigators confirmed that acts of abuse or neglect had actually occurred in 899,000 cases. In other words, investigators could substantiate less than one-third of the reports that they received. Some phone calls were false reports. Others concerned acts that did not meet the statutory definition for child abuse or neglect. For example, sometimes child welfare agencies receive calls from teenagers who feel their parents are neglectful, even if their parents do provide food, clothing, and shelter. At other times, a call may be the result of a misunderstanding. For example, a neighbor may phone about children who are home alone and may not realize that an adult is actually on the premises.

FINDING THE VICTIMS

"They almost looked as though they were sleeping. It almost looked like they were cuddled up together for the night." —Lt. Michael Fleming, commander of the Nassau, New York, homicide squad, after finding three young children dead in their bed after their mother killed them.

Quoted in Fox News.com, "Police Cite Possible Drowning, Poisoning in Deaths of 3 New York Children," February 25, 2008. www.foxnews.com/printer_friendly_story/ 0,3566,332390,00.html.

Although many reported cases of child abuse do not meet the legal definition for abuse, there are also many cases of abuse that would meet the definition but are never reported. Most cases of child abuse are not reported by anyone. For this reason, experts believe that the true number of cases each year probably is in the millions.

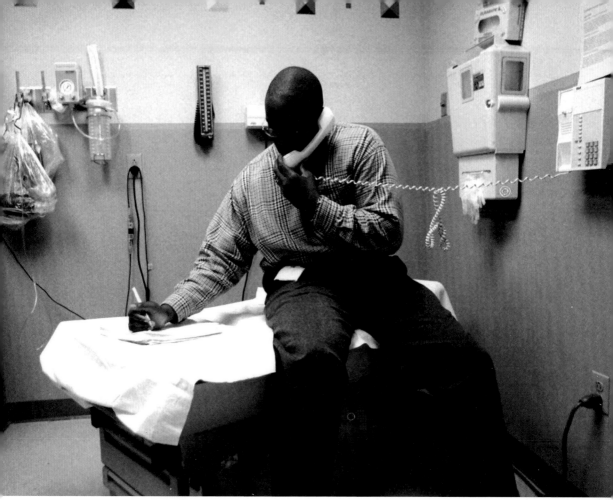

A Department of Children and Families social worker reports on a case of suspected child abuse from a Connecticut emergency room in 1998. Emergency room visits reveal only the most severe cases of child abuse.

The National Survey of Family Violence

Since most cases of child abuse are not reported, it is difficult to compile accurate statistics about how many children are actually abused or neglected. Up until the mid-1970s, statistics on violence in American families were based on reports that were made to child welfare agencies, police reports, and reports made by emergency room staff. But those statistics tended to underreport the actual number of abusive incidents. Most of the time, child abuse does not result in the police being called or in a child being taken to the doctor or to an emergency room. Most child abuse occurs behind closed doors, where concerned neighbors or family members are unlikely to see and report it. Most child abuse does not cause injuries that would be immediately obvious to teachers or child care workers. And the statistics collected by child welfare agencies only concern those cases where children were in enough danger that the state felt it was necessary to intervene. If researchers collect only data on those cases in which outside institutions such as police, child welfare organizations, or hospitals get involved, they end up with data on only the most severe cases of child abuse. They are left with no data about less severe cases.

In 1975 sociologists Richard Gelles and Murray Straus decided to try studying abuse in a new way. They wanted to have a large, national data sample. So they chose to interview people in every state. In addition, they wanted to find a way to collect data about how much abuse is really happening in American families. They did not think they could get that information just from police reports and child welfare agency statistics. They set up a new method. They went door to door, talking to random parents and caregivers in randomly chosen families nationwide. They asked parents and caregivers how they treated their children. They specifically asked about hitting children and about other acts of abuse. They also asked how adults in the family treated each other, which told them whether or not domestic violence was occurring. (In some states, causing a child to witness domestic violence is also considered an act of child abuse.)

It might seem unlikely that a person who abuses children would willingly tell a door-to-door surveyor about the abuse. But Straus and Gelles found that a surprisingly large number of parents and caregivers did tell interviewers about acts of abuse they had committed. Almost all parents admitted sometimes hitting their children as punishment. (Not everyone agrees with Straus and Gelles that hitting or spanking a child as punishment is a form of abuse. Spanking, also sometimes called corporal punishment, does not meet the legal definition for child abuse in most states, unless it becomes severe and extreme.) The family members interviewed by Straus and Gelles also admitted committing acts of severe abuse at times. Straus and Gelles defined extreme violence as including hitting with an object like a hairbrush or belt, kicking, punching, burning, and attacking with weapons. These sorts of acts would meet the statutory definition for physical abuse in most states.

According to the data gathered by Straus and Gelles, about 2.8 million children are likely to be seriously assaulted each year in the United States. As of the 2000 census, there were 72.3 million children in the United States. If Straus and Gelles are correct, a little less than 4 percent of American children are physically abused annually.

Neglect

Child abuse can take many different forms. The most common form is neglect. More than half of child abuse cases that are investigated by child protective services involve neglect. Neglect is

The most common form of child abuse is neglect, in which the parents fail to provide shelter, supervision, food, or medical care to their child.

defined differently in different states. In most states, it means depriving a child of food, clothing, shelter, medical care, or supervision. In twenty-one states, though, failure to educate a child also meets the legal definition for neglect.

Many neglect cases involve parents leaving their children unsupervised, often because the parents do not have child care available when they are working. Another common form of neglect is to expose children to illegal drugs. When a child's mother is a drug user, she may expose her child to drugs unintentionally by taking drugs while she is pregnant or breast-feeding. In some states, cases of prenatal and perinatal (just after birth) exposure to drugs make up a large percentage of the total reported child abuse for that state. In Illinois, for example, 40 percent of reported child abuse cases are reports of drug-exposed newborns.

However, there are also many neglect cases based on failure to feed and clothe children, failure to provide them with needed medical care, or failure to provide them with adequate shelter. New York social worker Marc Parent wrote about handling one such case. He received the following report:

> Mother lives alone with her five children—aged 2 yrs to 7 yrs. There is no furniture in the home. Children sleep on the floor and are frequently seen "running wild" in the hallways. The building is very run-down and there are drug dealers on every floor. The children are often seen naked and unsupervised. Unknown if there is food in the home now. Mother just had a baby and the infant appears to be thin and weak.[4]

In a case like this, child protection workers visit the home. They try to determine whether or not there is food in the house, whether or not the children have been fed regularly, whether they have been provided with clothing, and whether they are supervised. They must assess whether the parent is willing and able to care for the children in question. In many cases, parents and caregivers are trying their best to provide for their children. Sometimes they are overwhelmed by financial problems or the stress of caring for several children at once. In these cases, child

What Constitutes Child Abuse?

Different people have different ideas about what constitutes child abuse. Some people consider any corporal punishment of children to be abusive. Others only consider an action abusive if it is particularly harmful or injurious. For the state to intervene in family life, however, an act of abuse must meet the standards that are defined by law. Each state has its own laws defining what constitutes child abuse. In most states, any nonaccidental physical injury to a child is considered to be physical abuse. In fourteen states the law provides an exception for cases of corporal punishment if it is "reasonable" and does not cause an injury.

Neglect is usually defined as deprivation of food, clothing, shelter, medical care, or supervision. Eleven states, though, make exceptions for parents who are financially unable to provide for their children.

Almost all states include emotional abuse in their child abuse statutes. (Only Georgia and Washington do not.) Emotional abuse is usually defined as a psychological or emotional injury that results in anxiety, depression, withdrawal, or aggressive behavior.

Although different states have different laws, each state's laws must meet standards that are set by the federal government. These standards are defined by the Child Abuse Prevention and Treatment Act (CAPTA).

protection workers may be able to direct the family to community resources that can help. For example, they could help a single mother to apply for aid from the Women, Infants, and Children (WIC) program. WIC is a federal program that gives money to states. The money is used to provide food for children under the age of five and their mothers.

In some cases, neglect is caused by mental illness. While working in New York City, Parent also received this report:

Mother believes she and her children are under a hex. Mother is not feeding children because she is afraid of the food. The children are hungry now. Mother is behaving strangely. She is not answering the phone and will not open the door for anyone. Last week Mother reported seeing "strange men" outside of her apartment window.

Mother lives on the 16th floor. There are bizarre sounds coming from the apartment and it is believed that the children are at risk.[5]

When he visited this apartment, Parent and his partner found a single mother who genuinely loved and cared for her children but who was mentally ill. As the social workers talked with her, they discovered that she believed a hex would cause any food she brought into the house to become infested with shards of glass if it was not eaten right away. She was afraid to feed her children because she thought shards of glass were in the food. In that case, child protection workers took

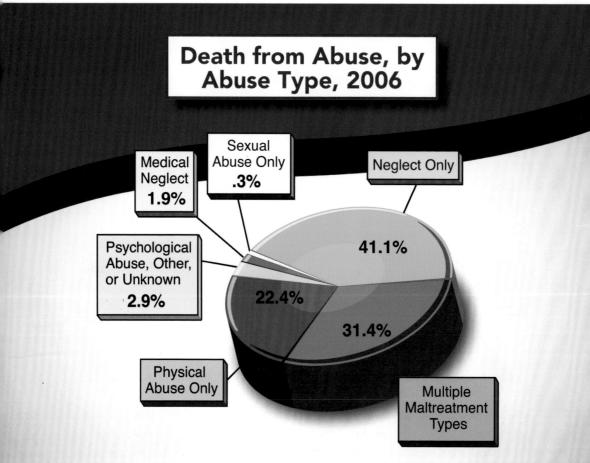

Death from Abuse, by Abuse Type, 2006

Medical Neglect
1.9%

Sexual Abuse Only
.3%

Neglect Only

Psychological Abuse, Other, or Unknown
2.9%

41.1%

22.4%

31.4%

Physical Abuse Only

Multiple Maltreatment Types

Source: Child Welfare Information Gateway. Available online at:
www.childwelfare.gov/pubs/factsheets/fatality.cfm#children.

temporary custody of the children, hoping that the children could be reunited with their mother after her mental illness was treated.

Physical Abuse

Neglect can take a physical toll on children. It may leave them malnourished, for example, and can cause developmental delays. But in cases of neglect, parents or caregivers may not actually intend to harm the children. They may simply fail to care for the children. They may not have enough money to buy food or clothes. They may be mentally ill. They might be addicted to alcohol or drugs. Or they may not understand how to care for a very young child.

Reacting to News of Abuse

"My sister's not crazy. She's not ballistic. This is a shock to all of us." —Robert McCord, reacting to news that his sister, Leatrice Brewer, had killed her three children.

Quoted in Fox News.com, "Police Cite Possible Drowning, Poisoning in Deaths of 3 New York Children," February 25, 2008. www.foxnews.com/printer_friendly_ story/0,3566,332390,00.html.

Nearly a third of child abuse cases, however, involve harm that was done to a child deliberately. In most states, a deliberate, nonaccidental injury to a child is considered physical abuse. Sexual acts forced on a child are always considered abusive, as well, even if they do not result in a visible injury. Thirty-six states also include threats of harm in their definitions for physical abuse. In addition, these states include, as part of their physical abuse definition, taking actions that risk harming a child, even if the child was not actually harmed. For example, forcing a child to sit on the windowsill of a twenty-story building is child abuse, even if the child does not fall and is not physically harmed. (Some states classify this kind of act as child endangerment.)

Nearly a third of child abuse cases involve deliberate physical harm or the threat of physical harm.

\ Physical abuse is less common than neglect, but it is easier for mandated child abuse reporters, such as doctors and nurses, to spot.\ Doctors and nurses become concerned about physical abuse when they see a child who has a pattern of injuries that have occurred regularly over a period of time. For example, they may see bruises or burns in different parts of the body, all in different stages of healing. When several injuries are all in different stages of healing, a doctor can surmise that the injuries occurred on several different occasions, not all at once.

Doctors can also recognize certain kinds of injuries as more likely than others to be the result of physical abuse. Children often injure themselves in the course of everyday life. But an injury caused by a fall, or by playing sports, will usually be located in a part of the body that is frequently exposed and not well protected. For example, typical childhood injuries might be located on the shins, knees, hands, elbows, nose, or forehead. Doctors are more suspicious if they see bruises on

False Accusations

Not all allegations of child abuse turn out to be true. In 2006 child welfare agencies received more than 3 million calls reporting possible cases of child abuse or neglect. Of those 3 million calls, nearly a million were in regard to behavior that is legal and not considered abuse. Of the original 3 million calls, only about 18 percent were found to concern verifiable cases of child abuse.

Every year, there are a few cases that are verified at first but are later discovered not to be true. In April 2003, Steve Smith was accusing of shaking his eleven-month-old, causing brain damage. His wife, Corinne, was shocked. She refused to believe that her husband could have abused their child. She insisted on further testing. The testing revealed that everyone in the family had von Willebrand disease, a disease that reduces blood clotting. People who have this disease can have major bruising and blood loss even from a minor fall. All the charges against Steve Smith were dropped.

the buttocks, thighs, torso, ears, or neck. They suspect child abuse if they see bruises shaped like a hand, belt buckle, electrical cord loop, or other object. Doctors also become suspicious if they find bruises on babies who have not yet learned to walk or to pull up and cruise. Babies that young are unlikely to hurt themselves accidentally.

One type of physical abuse that doctors have become expert at recognizing is shaken baby syndrome. Shaken baby syndrome is damage to a baby that is caused by shaking the baby. Babies who have been shaken tend to appear in the emergency room with bleeding inside their brains and eyes. They often have broken ribs as well. Babies with shaken baby syndrome are usually too young to walk or crawl. They are unlikely to have broken their own ribs or to have shaken their own heads hard enough to have caused internal bleeding. So emergency room workers can quickly figure out what must have happened.

For example, in 2008 doctors in a Summit County, Ohio, emergency room determined that three-month-old Camryn Jakeb Wilson was suffering from shaken baby syndrome. In Camryn's case, his mother, Crystal Wilson, had gone to an Alcoholics Anonymous meeting after arguing with her husband, Craig. Craig stayed home with Camryn. When Crystal arrived home, she found Camryn gasping for air in his baby swing. She rushed him to the emergency room, where he died. Doctors knew Camryn had likely been shaken because he had retinal hemorrhaging (bleeding in his eyes) and hemorrhaging in his brain. He also had broken ribs, some of which were new injuries and some of which were old. The old injuries established a pattern of abuse—someone in Camryn's family had been abusing him regularly.

Emotional Abuse—Is It Serious?

When people think about child abuse, they usually think about cases such as Camryn's—shaken baby syndrome, or other forms of physical abuse or neglect. But most states also include emotional abuse in their child abuse laws. Emotional abuse means failing to meet a child's emotional needs or causing a child to experience psychological damage. All forms of child abuse cause emotional and psychological damage. But some children are abused emotionally without having ever been injured physically.

What is emotional abuse? According to Patricia Leiby, a child abuse prevention coordinator in Frederick County, Maryland, "The child who constantly hears how dumb he is, or that

A cage used to confine a child is presented as evidence in a child abuse case. Caging a child is considered a form of emotional abuse.

he can't do it, is emotionally abused."[6] Most child abuse experts would probably agree with Leiby's definition. However, for emotional abuse to reach a point that would warrant intervention by state authorities, it must fall within the definition included in the laws of the state. State laws define emotional abuse much more narrowly. Most define it as psychological or emotional damage that leads to the development of a mental disorder such as anxiety or depression.

According to legal scholar J. Robert Shull, psychological abuse can consist of any "imaginative cruelty"[7] that does not involve physical injury or sexual abuse. Imaginative cruelty does not necessarily mean thinking of more creative but hurtful things to say to a child. It could also involve noninjurious physical acts such as confining a child by locking him or her in a closet or binding the child with ropes or chains. For example, in Lancaster, Pennsylvania, Elsa Speller locked her thirteen-year-old daughter naked in a closet for seventeen hours. She provided a bucket for a toilet but gave the girl no food or water. Patricia Muncy of La Grande, Oregon, chained her thirteen-year-old daughter to a tree for two days.

Psychological injury can also be caused by a pattern of verbally belittling or denigrating a child. (Parents may occasionally, or even regularly, criticize their children without it being considered child abuse, however.) It can mean damaging a child's personal possessions or humiliating the child in front of friends. Or it could involve threatening a child's pet or deliberately hurting or killing a pet while forcing the child to watch. In families that are experiencing domestic violence or spousal abuse, a child might be emotionally injured by being forced to watch his or her mother being hurt or threatened.

Is emotional abuse as serious as physical abuse and neglect? Most child abuse experts consider emotional abuse to be far more damaging—and far more common—than physical abuse. Psychologists James Garbarino, Edna Guttman, and Janis Wilson Seeley write: "Children are resilient, and they can handle parents' normal emotional ebb and flow; what most children typically cannot handle is a pervasive pattern of destructive emotions or extreme outbursts that threaten their world. Isolated trauma is not nearly so threatening as repeated emotional assault."[8]

In other words, it is easier for children to recover from the physical damage of an assault that occurs on rare occasions than it is for them to live with constant belittling, name-calling, and intimidation. Unfortunately, many abused children must recover from both.

CHAPTER 2

WHEN DOES CHILD ABUSE HAPPEN?

"My mother drank heavily," remembers Denise (not her real name), a child abuse survivor who grew up to be an attorney. "I've never been sure whether it was deliberate, or whether she was just so blind drunk she didn't realize what she was doing, but she burned me with a lit cigarette. And I can still remember that pain."[9]

Denise's mother was an alcoholic. Two-year-old Benjamin Metz-Johnson's mother, Carrie Metz, was addicted to a different substance: heroin. She was taking methadone, a prescription drug used to wean addicts off heroin. Metz chose to keep her methadone in a toddler-sized sippy cup on the counter of her kitchen. In January 2007 Benjamin grabbed a bottle of methadone, which is extremely toxic for young children, off Metz's counter. Metz later testified that she did not believe Benjamin had ingested any of the methadone, so she did not take him to a doctor. A few hours later, he turned blue and stopped breathing. Then he died. Metz was charged and convicted of child neglect and sentenced to six years in prison.

Every Kind of Home

Denise and Benjamin's stories could have come from any family in any home in America. In fact, though, Denise grew up in an affluent, two-parent family in a suburb of Boston. Benjamin was the son of a struggling single mother in Kenosha, Wisconsin. Child abuse can occur in any kind of home. It occurs in wealthy families, middle-class families, and poor families. Abuse is committed by people of every race, gender, ethnicity, religion, and sexual orientation.

Alcoholics and drug addicts, like Denise's and Benjamin's mothers, are more likely than the average person to abuse a child. Children of drug- or alcohol-addicted parents are three times more likely to be abused and four times more likely to be neglected than children of nonaddicted parents. But many children are also abused by adults who do not drink or take drugs. And there are many alcoholics who do not abuse their children.

Similarly, many child abusers were abused themselves as children. A history that includes being the victim of abuse puts

Drug addicts are more likely to abuse their children.

a person at a very slightly increased chance of abusing children himself or herself. But most survivors of child abuse do not grow up to become child abusers themselves. Most cannot imagine subjecting other children to the experiences that they themselves endured.

The Typical Perpetrator

Perpetrator is a term used by law enforcement agencies to describe the person who committed a crime or an act of wrongdoing. In some ways, it is correct to say that there is no typical

Most perpetrators of child abuse are young parents who are living at or below poverty level, such as this homeless mother shown with her two sons.

case of child abuse. Each family is different, each child is different, and each caregiver is different. However, even though child abuse occurs in all kinds of families, child welfare authorities see certain trends in the cases in which they are asked to intervene.

A HORRIFIC OUTCOME

"Perhaps each person present has his or her own private opinion about what occurred across the street. . . . To some it was a flagrant example of abuse, to others a very unfortunate accident. To some it was the result of parents who were overstressed, without resources and respite. To others it was the horrific outcome of a frightening need for power and control. But no matter where you are on this issue, the bottom line is this: No one, no one should die the way Calista Springer did." —Karin Orr, pastor, Centreville United Methodist Church.

Quoted in Kathy Jessup, "'God Was There with Calista': St. Joseph County Residents Attend Vigil to Remember 16-Year-Old Who Died in Fire," *Kalamazoo Gazette*, August 28, 2008. http://blog.mlive.com/kzgazette_impact/2008/08/god_was_there_with_calista_st/print.html.

Most perpetrators of child abuse and neglect are young adults. They are typically in their mid-twenties but had their first child before the age of eighteen. Most do not have a high school diploma and have not completed any higher education such as college or vocational school. Most are living at or below the poverty level. Frequently, perpetrators of abuse and neglect are depressed and have difficulty coping with stress in their lives. Many have been the victims of violence themselves.

Almost all perpetrators of child abuse and neglect have one thing in common. They are people who are responsible for caring for and supervising children. In 2006 more than 75 percent of perpetrators of child abuse and neglect were the parents of the victims. About 15 percent were nonparent caretakers, such as day care providers, babysitters, and relatives. Another 10 percent were abused by unknown perpetrators. In those cases, children were unable or unwilling to identify their abusers, and investigators were not able to identify the perpetrators.

Men and women are equally likely to commit acts of child abuse and neglect. But the type of abuse they commit varies by gender. The most common type of abuse, neglect, is usually committed by mothers. Violence and physical abuse are most commonly committed by fathers or by male caretakers.

The Atypical Perpetrator

A parent or caregiver does not have to be mentally ill to commit an act of child abuse. Most commonly, a child abuser is angry, frustrated, overwhelmed, or otherwise overcome with negative emotions. But in some cases, parents are mentally ill. These parents may commit acts of abuse without fully realizing what they are doing. For example, in New York City, social worker Marc Parent received a report about a mother who had thrown two of her children out a twenty-third story window. The mother said she was trying to send her children to God, to save them "from the sins of this world."[10]

Most parents who have mental disorders do not abuse their children. But mental illness increases a parent's risk of committing abuse or neglect. The risk is highest in parents who have been diagnosed with a severe mental illness, such as schizophrenia or major depression. Schizophrenia, for example, can cause a person to have hallucinations and delusions and to hear voices. It can make parents confused about their surroundings or about how best to keep their children safe, even if they genuinely love and care for their children. Depression, by contrast, may make parents more likely to neglect their children, simply by making it harder for parents to function normally. Some depressed parents find it difficult even to get out of bed in the morning. It is hard for them, therefore, to deal with feeding and caring for a young child.

Researchers believe that people with mental disorders can still be good parents to their children. But they also believe these parents may need extra support. For example, they may need parenting classes or counseling. Many need financial support, especially to pay for health care. And they may have an even greater need than many other parents do for financial assistance to help them pay for child care and housing.

Typical Victims of Neglect

Perpetrators of neglect may believe that they are very different from people who physically abuse children. However, neglect can be just as hard on a child as physical abuse. For example, on August 13, 2008, a neighbor reported hearing screaming coming from the home of Jon Pomeroy and Rebecca Long in

If parents cannot afford child care, they may leave their children at home alone when they go to work even if the children are too young to be left alone.

Carnation, Washington. A sheriff's deputy visited and found Pomeroy's fourteen-year-old daughter near death from malnutrition. Pomeroy and Long had restricted her to half a Dixie cup of water per day. At night, they made her sleep in their bedroom and slid a heavy dresser in front of the door to keep her from sneaking out. Pomeroy's daughter had a history of sneaking out of her bedroom at night to drink out of the toilet bowl, because she was afraid her parents would hear the water running if she used the faucet.

REMOVING CHILDREN

"As the system is now, we end up removing children when they could remain safely at home if we had the appropriate services to offer them. We often intervene with a sword when a scalpel would do." —Helen Jones-Kelley, executive director, Montgomery County, Ohio, Children's Services.

Quoted in Pew Commission on Children in Foster Care, "Fostering the Future: Safety, Permanence and Well-Being for Children in Foster Care," May 18, 2004. http://pewfoster care.org/press/files/transcript051804.pdf.

When she was found, Pomeroy's daughter was badly dehydrated and emaciated. She was 4 feet 7 inches tall (140cm) and weighed 48 pounds (22kg). Her teeth were beginning to fall out from malnutrition. The sheriff's deputy who found her rushed her to Seattle Children's Hospital, where she remained for two weeks.

Gregory Jones and Jessica Lee Lovell of Jackson, Mississippi, had two children, a five-month-old and a sixteen-month-old. Both had been born prematurely and needed to see a doctor regularly. When Jones and Lovell stopped taking their children to their doctor, he feared for the children's lives. He phoned the police and reported that the children might be in danger. When child protective investigators arrived at their home, they discovered that the children were badly malnourished and dehydrated. Investigators called an ambulance and took the children to the hospital. Jones and Lovell were charged with child endangerment for neglecting to feed their children.

Cases of neglect, like those of Pomeroy and Long or Jones and Lovell, are the most common type of child abuse in the United States. Neglect is three times more common than physical abuse. Children are much more likely to be neglected if they are living in poverty. According to researchers at the Children's Defense Fund, nearly 13 million American children were living in poverty in 2005. In families with a total yearly income of less than fifteen thousand dollars, the children are twenty-two times more likely to be abused or neglected than the children in families with total yearly incomes of thirty thousand dollars or more.

Why are children living in poverty more likely to be neglected? Sometimes parents do not have the resources they need to take adequate care of their children. A common example is a single mother of a four-year-old and a six-year-old who works the night shift. Having no child care, she may tuck her children into bed at night and go to work, hoping for the best. But leaving young children without adequate supervision is a form of neglect.

Even though poverty increases a child's chances of being abused, most poor parents and caregivers do not neglect the children in their care. Out of the nearly 13 million children living in poverty in the United States in 2005, fewer than 1 million were abused or neglected. And not all of those 1 million abuse and neglect victims came from poor families.

A Typical Victim of Physical Abuse

At about 9:20 P.M. on a Sunday evening in August 2008, Michael Below, a new father in West Bend, Wisconsin, became frustrated with his two-month-old daughter. She would not stop crying. Her mother was at work. Later, Below told investigators that he picked the baby up by her feet and began banging her head against her diaper-changing table. Investigators noted, "On a scale of one to 10, 10 being the hardest, defendant hit [the baby's] head on the changing table about eight or nine."[11] Pretending that nothing was wrong, Below took the baby with him when he went to pick up her mother from work at 10 P.M.

But the baby was breathing strangely, and her mother became frightened. She called an ambulance. On admission at Children's Hospital of Wisconsin, the baby was found to have severe brain injuries, bleeding in her eyes, a skull fracture, and brain swelling. Those injuries had occurred that evening. But doctors also found older injuries: broken ribs and an older area of bleeding in her brain.

A one-year-old child abuse victim with circular burn marks down the spine. Toddlers are most at risk for physical abuse.

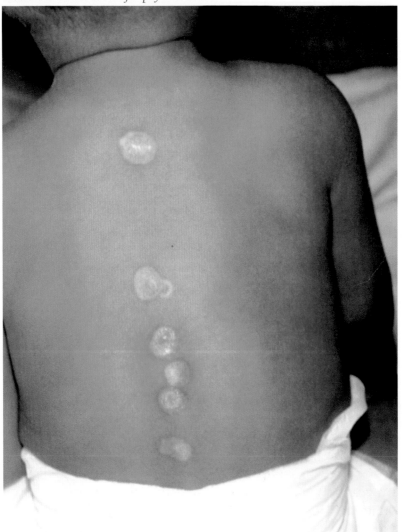

Runaways and Throwaways

Child abuse is one of the most common reasons why children end up living on the street, homeless. Around 20 percent of children who run away from home say that they have run away in order to escape physical abuse at home. According to the National Runaway Switchboard, one-seventh of U.S. children run away from home at least once before they reach the age of eighteen.

"Throwaway" children are children whose families have thrown them out. Among throwaway children, the incidence of abuse and neglect is even higher than it is among runaways. Researchers who sifted through runaway hotline calls from 2000 to 2005 found that about 25 percent of throwaway children who phoned a hotline had been neglected. About 14 percent had been physically abused.

When investigators asked Below what had happened, he told them that he was under a lot of stress. He was worried about his finances. Investigators noted in their report that "he does not know what got over him, that he just lost control and was frustrated."[12]

Below's story is an example of the next most common type of child abuse—physical abuse. Unlike neglect, which is associated more with families living in poverty, physical abuse is just as likely to occur in wealthy families as it is in poor families. It is a little more common in families that have experienced a divorce, separation, and/or remarriage, however. The children who are most at risk for physical abuse are the very young, especially children who are under age three. Teens are the next most commonly abused age group. But children ages four to twelve are also frequently abused. Boys are more likely to be beaten, while girls are more likely to be sexually assaulted.

The most at-risk children are those who are especially hard to care for. This group includes, for example, children who had low birth weights or who were premature, like Jones and Lovell's children. It also includes children who are physically disabled or developmentally delayed. It is especially easy for an abuser to

Death from Abuse, by Age, 2006

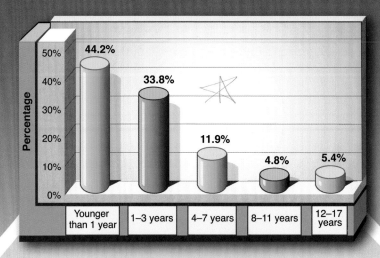

Source: Child Welfare Information Gateway. Available online at:
www.childwelfare.gov/pubs/factsheets/fatality.cfm#children.

overpower a child who is unusually small, weak, or disabled. When these children grow older and stronger, sometimes the abuse decreases because the abuser is afraid of being hit back. As babies, though, children do not hit back. What they can do is cry. But crying may trigger some caregivers to become angry and violent.

Some child welfare advocates find that children in families that have only one or two children are more at risk than children in larger families. This may be because when older children are present, they may step in to try to protect younger children from abuse. In some cases older children will stand between a caregiver and a younger sibling, trying to protect the younger sibling. But more often, older children simply step in and help with child care. As a result, the younger children in the family spend less time with a parent who might abuse them. This helps to keep the younger children in the family safe. But it also forces older children to grow up much more quickly. In these families, older children may feel like little adults, caring for children before they have become adults themselves.

Homicides

In most cases child abuse is not fatal. Unfortunately, though, sometimes children do die from abuse. Sometimes they die of injuries caused by physical abuse. They may also die of neglect if they are extremely malnourished or have been denied medical care. In rare cases, they can die from what would normally be considered a kind of emotional abuse—being confined to a small area. In 2008 sixteen-year-old Calista Springer, of Centreville, Michigan, died in a house fire. Her parents had chained her to her bed—a form of emotional abuse. But then the house caught fire, and she was unable to escape. She died in the blaze. Springer's mother later pleaded no contest to charges of child neglect, and Springer's sisters were taken from the family and placed in the care of relatives.

The burned remains of the home in which Calista Springer died.

In 2005 authorities were aware of 1,460 children in the United States who died as a result of injuries caused by abuse. Experts believe, though, that more than half of fatalities caused by child abuse are not classified as abuse. Instead, they may be recorded as accidents. In the United States, almost 2 children out of every 100,000 die each year from physical abuse.

Homicide cases are not particularly different from other child abuse cases, except that they involve a death. The perpetrators of homicide cases share the same characteristics as the perpetrators of nonfatal abuse. As in other child abuse cases, the perpetrators of child homicides are usually the parent or caregiver. Parents and caregivers perpetrate more than 76 percent of child homicides. In another 13 percent of cases, the perpetrator is someone else the child knew, such as a nonparent caretaker (like a day care provider or a nanny).

Sometimes the perpetrator in a homicide is someone that most people would not think of, like a sibling. For example, New York City social worker Marc Parent was called to investigate a case that was expected to end in a fatality. A five-year-

Shaken Babies

Every year about fourteen hundred babies in the United States are killed or injured by caregivers who become frustrated with the demands of baby care and shake their babies. About a quarter of these babies die of their injuries. Eighty percent of babies who survive shaking are permanently disabled. They may have severe brain damage and may develop cerebral palsy or become mentally retarded. Some babies are so seriously injured that they are never able to breathe on their own. They must depend on a respirator. Some babies are left blind or unable to feel touch. These children need constant medical attention.

Some babies do survive shaking and go on to recover. These children are able to lead a relatively normal life. Even in these cases, though, children often have behavior problems. They have a hard time controlling sudden impulses and may find it difficult to organize their work or to concentrate in school.

old boy was in a coma, and his four-year-old brother had been hospitalized as well. At first, the social workers believed that the children's mother or aunt was responsible for the injuries. But as they investigated, they realized that the children's nine-year-old babysitter, their cousin, had beaten them.

Although the perpetrators of child abuse homicides match the perpetrators of other forms of child abuse, the victims are slightly different. Nonfatal child abuse tends to target very young children and teenagers. But fatal child abuse predominantly affects very young children. Young children are more vulnerable to violence than older children, and they may die from acts that would not kill an older child.

Babies and preschoolers are at the highest risk for being killed by their parents or caretakers. When that happens, it often happens in the first few weeks of the child's life. Sometimes unwanted newborns are killed by their mothers. At other times, mothers abandon babies in public places, where they may be rescued or may freeze or starve to death before a rescue occurs.

Preschool children, on the other hand, are often killed when their parents or caretakers try to control their behavior. They are also killed when parents or caregivers become angry in response to normal preschool behavior, such as crying, hitting, not using the bathroom, or getting dirty. Parents may react to such behavior by throwing the child against a hard surface or by hitting or smothering the child. They may not intend to kill the child but may not realize how fragile a very young child can be.

A Safe Haven

To children and adults who have not had to live with abuse or neglect, stories of abused children sound horrific. But children who live through abuse may not realize that there is anything unusual about their family lives. To them, abuse and neglect are not an aberration but are a normal condition of everyday life. They may not mention the abuse to friends or to caring adults. They may feel afraid that they will not be believed, or they may have been wrongly told by their abusers that the abuse is their own fault.

For children to recover from this kind of life, they need something more than a safe place to live and grow. They need an environment in which they are encouraged to develop their own interests and in which they can begin to believe that they deserve to be happy. Frequently, child welfare workers are able to work with a child's family to help the family become a place where children can thrive and be happy. At other times, the original family is so unsafe that children must be placed in another family. Either way, the state monitors the children to make sure that they are well cared for and remain safe.

How Is Child Abuse Investigated?

In October 2007 a Mesa, Arizona, five-year-old told her teacher that her father and stepmother had been beating her. The teacher took the girl to the school nurse, who documented nearly one hundred bruises on the girl's back, legs, arms, buttocks, and chest. Teachers and school nurses are required to report cases of suspected child abuse, so they phoned the Mesa police.

Mesa police officers went to the girl's home and interviewed her parents. Her father, Ezra Hazell, explained that he customarily beat her if she was disobedient or if she did not do her homework. He told police that he and Kirstie Hazell, the girl's stepmother, would have their five-year-old hold a push-up position. He said they would put a book on the floor in front of her, and if she did not pay attention to the book or missed a word, they would beat her several times with a belt. Ezra Hazell also told investigators that he sometimes beat his daughter with a computer cord. The Mesa police investigators were appalled by Hazell's story. Later they told newspaper reporters that it was one of the worst cases of child abuse they had ever seen. Hazell and his wife were arrested. Their children were placed in the care of relatives. Eventually, Ezra Hazell was sentenced to eight months in jail and ten years of probation. Kirstie Hazell was sentenced to ten years of probation.

Mandated Reporters

In the Hazell case, the child herself reported her own abuse. But child welfare agencies accept reports of child abuse from anyone. A neighbor, a family member, or a child's friend can pick up the phone and call a child abuse hotline. An abused child can even call on his or her own behalf. For example, anyone can phone the Childhelp National Child Abuse Hotline (800-422-4453). The hotline is staffed seven days a week, twenty-four hours a day. Or they could phone the local department of children and family services or the police.

However, although anyone may report abuse, people who work in certain jobs are required to report abuse. They do not

A teacher examines a scrape on a young girl's arm. Teachers are part of a group of mandated reporters—those who must report suspected child abuse.

have to be certain that abuse occurred. They only have to suspect it. People who are required by law to report suspected abuse are called mandated reporters. The Hazell case was reported when the abused girl told her story to two mandated reporters—her teacher and the school nurse. Doctors, dentists, social workers, counselors, police officers, and day care providers are also mandated reporters. Mandated reporters must usually report suspected child abuse right away by making a phone call. Then they are required to follow up within a day or so with a written report.

When child welfare agencies receive a report of abuse, they must assess it. This means that they must decide whether the report is likely to concern a case of child abuse or not. It also means they must determine whether or not they have enough information to find out more. For example, a community member might phone to report abuse that was observed in the grocery store or on a bus or train. But child welfare investigators may not have enough information to follow up on this kind of report. They may not have names or addresses, for example. Investigators also must screen out calls that do not have anything to do with child abuse. For example, they may get phone calls from people who disagree with a parent's choices about how late to let a teenager stay out at night. Or they may get phone calls from people who are concerned about a drug-addicted child. In response to that kind of call, investigators would refer the caller to a community agency that offers substance abuse or rehabilitation programs.

Immediate Danger

In the end, investigators usually screen out about one-third of reports of child abuse. They follow up on the other two-thirds of abuse reports. Because child welfare agencies have limited staff, though, they cannot always follow up right away. Instead, they try to focus on the cases in which a child is thought to be in immediate danger. Of course, it is impossible for investigators to know, prior to conducting an investigation, which children are actually in immediate danger.

A social worker pays a visit to an apartment to determine whether child abuse has occurred there. An important part of a social worker's job is to evaluate the home to determine if it is a safe environment for children.

To help them assess the danger, investigators consider the elements of abuse mentioned by the original caller. If the caller said that the child had many injuries and that all of the injuries were different (for example, a burn, bruises, and a broken bone), or if the injuries were all to the face and head, investigators feel they should respond more quickly. Likewise, if a child is thought to be home alone or in need of immediate medical attention or is alleged to be badly malnourished, child protection workers try to go to the scene immediately. Investigators also respond immediately if they hear that a caregiver is behaving bizarrely or is under the influence of drugs or alcohol.

Interviewing Children

Once investigators determine that a report is real and should be investigated, they must interview the child who is alleged to have been abused. The investigators' first priority at this point is still to find out if the child is in any immediate danger. But they must also try to reassure the child. Counselor Connie Carnes notes: "It is very important for the interviewer . . . to stay attuned to the child's psychological state during the interview. Because the last thing we would want to do is to retraumatize the child by the way that we interview them."[13]

It is not always easy for investigators to convince children to talk to them. Children may love their parents and caregivers deeply even if they are being abused or neglected. They usually do not want to say anything critical about their parents, relatives, or other caregivers. Sometimes they are afraid that they will get in trouble if they say anything. David Pelzer told his teacher, Miss Moss, and his school principal, Mr. Hansen. He remembers being interviewed about his mother's abuse:

> The police officer explains why Mr. Hansen called him. I can feel myself shrink into the chair. The officer asks that I tell him about Mother. I shake my head no. Too many people already know the secret, and I know she'll find

Due Process of Law

Some critics of the child welfare system argue that oftentimes children are removed without due process of law. *Due process* is a legal term. It means that an accused person is not assumed to be guilty but instead must have the opportunity to defend himself or herself by presenting evidence and witnesses in court. Some parents argue that they have been subjected to a full-scale children's services investigation just on the basis of a phone call from a neighbor. These parents argue that even if children are not removed from the home, parents are still exposed to the embarrassment of having investigators ask family members, friends, neighbors, and teachers about the possibility of abuse.

Virginia mother Cari Clark says that her name was listed on the Virginia state registry of child abusers/neglectors simply because her neighbor called the state to report that one of Clark's children was walking unsupervised in the neighborhood. "It's not like calling a cop when there's a noisy party," Clark explains. "They don't just send someone around to say hey, cool it. It's a full-scale investigation that can turn a family's life inside out."

Quoted in David Wagner, "Child Removal Lacks Due Process," *Insight on the News*, November 24, 1997, p. 22.

out. A soft voice calms me. I think it's Miss Moss. She tells me it's all right. I take a deep breath, wring my hands and reluctantly tell them about Mother and me. Then the nurse has me stand up and show the policeman the scar on my chest. Without hesitation, I tell them it was an accident; which it was—Mother never meant to stab me.[14]

Investigators also interview the child's parents or guardians, as well as the person or persons who are thought to have committed the abuse. Sometimes parents who have physically abused their kids understand that what they did was wrong and illegal. They try to cover it up by lying about how the child received the injuries. They may say that the child fell or that the injuries came from playing sports. Other parents do not understand the difference between corporal punishment and abuse. These parents may be very honest with investigators, as Ezra Hazell was. They may tell investigators exactly what they did and come up with a reason why they thought their actions were justified by the child's behavior.

LIVING IN FOSTER CARE

"Children need the grounding of a permanent home. You don't get that in foster care. You get it in a family. In the last year we met a lot of kids of foster care, and they broke our hearts. One young man said that the thing—the first thing that he did every day when he got home from school was to check whether his belongings had been packed. We met a young woman who learned from an early age to carry her school records with her so that every time she moved to a new foster home in a new school district she could show the principal what grades she should be in. We met twin sisters who spent their whole childhood apart from each other because they were put in different foster homes. They used to run away just to see each other and spend time together. No child should have to do that." —William Gray, vice chairman, Pew Commission on Children in Foster Care.

Quoted in Pew Commission on Children in Foster Care, "Fostering the Future: Safety, Permanence and Well-Being for Children in Foster Care," May 18, 2004. http://pew fostercare.org/press/files/transcript051804.pdf.

A social worker questions a young boy about his broken arm. Social workers must be very careful when interviewing children since victims of child abuse are often reluctant to talk about their experiences.

While investigators interview the parents or caregivers and the children, they also assess the condition of the family home. They try to determine whether the home is a safe environment and take time to interview friends and neighbors who know the family. Investigators also review any paperwork that is connected with the family. They find out if there have been allegations of child abuse or neglect before. They review each child's medical history and any criminal history that the parents or caregivers may have. They also review school files for each child in the family.

In the end, investigators will classify each case of potential child abuse as substantiated or unsubstantiated. A substantiated case is one in which most of the evidence suggests that abuse probably did occur. Investigators can classify a case as substantiated even if they do not have enough evidence to convict an abuser in court. If they classify the case as unsubstantiated, it means that they could not find enough evidence to convince themselves that abuse really occurred. In 2006 about 18 percent of child abuse reports in the United States were found to be substantiated.

Families Who Need Help

In many cases investigators find families who may not have abused or neglected their children but whom the investigators think are at risk for abuse or neglect. For example, sometimes a doctor thinks, but is not certain, that a child is being neglected. The child might not be as tall or weigh as much as the norm for his or her age, but that alone would not prove neglect. Some children are naturally small or thin. Also, some parents feed a child less because of poverty but provide as much food as they can with the financial resources that they have. If parents are trying their best to take care of their children but fail to do so only because of poverty, many states will grant them an exception to charges of neglect. In about one-third of states, if a family does not feed its children, it is only considered neglect if the parents knew about food assistance programs and deliberately chose not to use them. In cases where families simply need financial help to provide for children, investigators would put the family in touch with resources in the community. For example, mothers of children under age five can get food checks from the WIC program.

If investigators suspect that children are in danger because of neglect and not just poverty, they can arrange to have the family visited at home by a doctor, nurse, or social worker. They can also have doctors schedule frequent follow-up appointments for children or arrange for the family to have a consultation with a social worker.

A Chance for Something More

"Having my own place is like breaking a chain. I am the first one in my family to own a house. . . . Without DCFS, I wouldn't have this job, I wouldn't be able to save all that money. If it wasn't for the foster care system, I don't know where I would have been. I could have been living on the streets. Being in the system gave me all these opportunities. I just did what I could with those opportunities." —David Torrez, former foster child.

Quoted in Los Angeles County Department of Children and Family Services, "Our Stories." http://dcfs.co.la.us/aboutus/brochure_our_stories.pdf.

Investigators also see cases of physical abuse that may fall into a gray area. In some cases, parents who mean to discipline their children have used corporal punishment that became too extreme. Sometimes investigators believe that parents are trying their best and that the abuse was an isolated incident. They may feel that the child is not in any immediate danger. In cases like this, they may arrange for the family to receive some support from community resources. For example, they might arrange for parents to take parenting classes to help them learn other ways to discipline children that do not involve corporal punishment. Or they might arrange for regular home visits from a nurse or social worker.

Documenting Abuse and Neglect

If investigators can substantiate that abuse or neglect definitely occurred, the next step is to preserve the evidence. This usually means taking the child to see a doctor or nurse for a physical exam. The evidence of child abuse and neglect is usually best documented by a doctor or nurse. In cases where neglect is suspected, doctors can evaluate whether a child is developing normally for his or her age. Blood tests can show whether a child is getting enough of certain nutrients, such as iron.

Evidence of child abuse is best documented by a doctor or nurse.

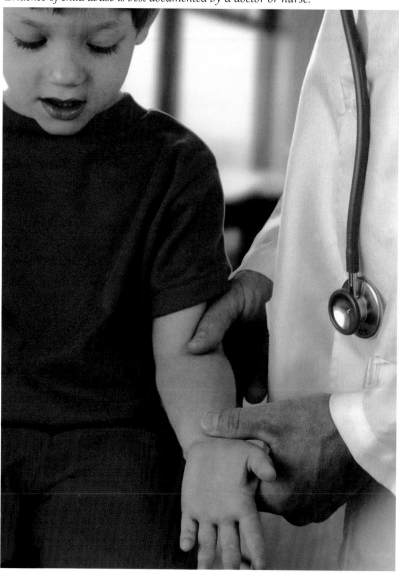

In cases where investigators suspect physical abuse, doctors can evaluate whether a child's physical injuries seem to be normal for the child's age and typical activities. For example, babies who have not learned to walk rarely bruise themselves. Older children who do run around and fall frequently are still unlikely to bruise themselves in well-protected parts of the body. For example, children do not usually bruise their upper arms, upper legs, neck, or buttocks in an accidental fall. If children have been burned, doctors suspect that the burn happened deliberately if it is very symmetrical.

When doctors find injuries that are suspicious, doctors or investigators need to take photographs. Photographs are important because later, lawyers representing the child can include the photos as exhibits in their legal documents. The photos may be important if the state asks a judge to issue a restraining order preventing an abusive caregiver from having contact with a child.

Medical guidelines for documenting child abuse say that doctors should take color pictures of each injury from at least two angles, including a ruler or coin in the picture so that it is clear how large or small the injury is. Although it is important legally to have this proof of a child's injuries, the process of taking photographs can be very hard on children. Social worker Marc Parent remembers watching two detectives take photos of a child's bruises. He writes:

> Two oddball-looking detectives were working Davey over with the largest, most awkward-looking camera I'd ever seen. It was a tangled monstrosity in three huge pieces that looked more suited for 1930s medical procedures than for taking pictures. It took the two of them to operate it—poorly. They stretched the reluctant Davey prostrate on a white table to photograph close-ups of his ripening bruises. . . . They'd have Davey freeze in the most impossible display of his injuries as they moved in close with the camera only to find the flash units hadn't charged. Davey would strain to hold his position as the men waited for what seemed like an eternity, through the whine of the recharging dinosaurs. The child winced

and whimpered as they began, but by the time they'd finished, he had closed his eyes and let them have their way, assuming the wayward positions they put him in like he'd done it a thousand times.[15]

Voluntary Services

Child welfare investigators are required by law to avoid removing children from their families if they possibly can. Most states require investigators to make what are called "reasonable efforts" to keep families together. There are two reasons for this. First, states recognize that parents have a right to raise their own children without interference from the government unless something unusual, such as an extreme case of abuse or neglect, has occurred. Second, research shows that children are better off with their families unless they are in immediate danger. It used to be more common for investigators to remove children from families, especially if parents were addicted to drugs or alcohol. But recent studies have shown that even babies who are born to drug-addicted mothers fare better if they remain with their mothers while the mothers go through a substance abuse rehabilitation program. Not only are the babies better off staying with their mothers, but the mothers are more likely to complete a rehab program when they have their babies with them.

To keep families together, investigators will make a safety plan. They give the family the option to accept voluntary services. (Voluntary services are those that a family is not required by law or by a court order to participate in.) They try to identify resources that will help the family with its unique set of stresses. For example, if parents have a substance abuse problem, investigators can arrange for them to go through rehab or to go to Alcoholics Anonymous meetings. If parents need help learning parenting skills, they can attend parenting classes. Investigators also often arrange for families to receive regular home visits from social workers or visiting nurses. They may arrange free child care for the family. They may also arrange for members of the family to receive health care for mental or physical illnesses. Visits from social workers often help to motivate parents and caregivers to be more aware of how they treat their children.

Removing Children

In some cases, though, investigators feel they must remove children from their homes for the children's own safety. Even if an investigation does not substantiate a charge of child abuse, children may be removed from their homes if conditions in the home are unsafe. In the best of cases, children are placed with family members, such as grandparents, aunts, uncles, and adult siblings. This kind of foster care is called kinship care. If no family member is willing or able to take the children, however, they

Parents visit their baby daughter in the hospital; because the baby tested positive for cocaine, she is being placed in foster care.

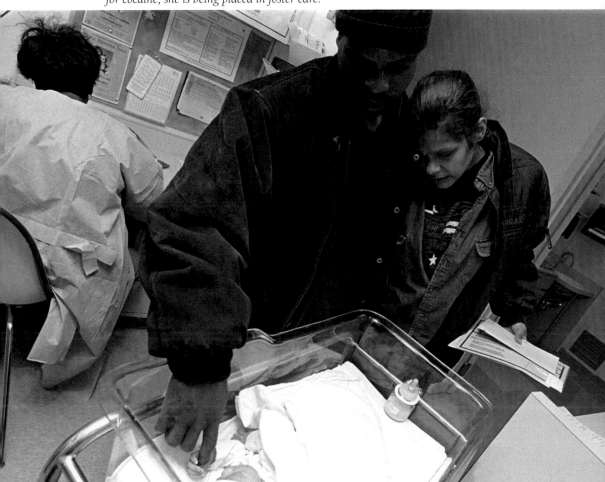

SOS Mothers separated Help

In 2008 Texas Protective Services and law enforcement investigated allegations of child abuse at a communal polygamist ranch operated by the Fundamentalist Church of Jesus Christ of Latter Day Saints. They separated the mothers from the children for over a month before determining that there was no basis for charges.

must be placed with a foster family they are not related to or in a group home.

For example, April Smith was the thirty-two-year-old mother of three children: a sixteen-month-old, a four-year-old, and a twelve-year-old. Investigators visiting her home found it littered with broken glass, animal and human feces, moldy food, and hazardous electrical fixtures. Smith and her boyfriend were addicted to drugs. They sometimes left home for days, leaving the twelve-year-old to babysit both her younger siblings and a pair of unrelated seven-year-olds. When they were home, Smith's boyfriend abused her in front of the children. (Many states have laws stating that forcing children to watch their mother being abused is a form of emotional abuse.) The twelve-year-old had tried to commit suicide and was doing badly in school. In this case, child welfare investigators removed the children from the home.

It seemed obvious to social workers that Smith's home was not a suitable environment for children. But investigators also realized that removing the children and placing them in foster care was not ideal either. They were not able to place all three children in the same foster home.

There are also times when children are removed from their families even though authorities know that the parent has not done anything wrong. In these cases, investigators believe that the parents, while not abusive, may not be able to protect children from the abuse of someone else in the family or neighborhood. Marc Parent, reflecting on his experience as a social worker in New York City, recalled a case in which doctors at an emergency room determined that an eight-year-old girl was being raped regularly. She lived with her mother and younger siblings, and investigators were able to determine that her mother had done nothing wrong. Social workers spent hours trying to determine who the rapist was, keeping the family safe at the hospital in the meantime. But they could not find out who was abusing the girl, and they believed that if they sent her home, the rapes would continue. They did not believe that the girl's mother, even though she had done nothing wrong, would be able to protect her, or any of her siblings, from being abused again. Finally, they decided to take the children into temporary custody. Parent describes what happened next:

> Security closed in on the family, and as they did, Lucia [the children's mother] screamed something in Spanish and the four of them bolted to the far wall, knocking

through trays, stretchers, and equipment. Alex and I followed them quickly along with security and cornered
them together where the children crouched down to the
floor, rolling themselves into a tight ball around their
mother. . . . The ball grew tighter as we closed in; each
of the kids wrapping their fists around whatever clothing
on their mother they could find. . . .

It took every single guard to split it apart. . . . Many
of the nurses looked away. You know it's bad when the
ER staff looks away. One by one the screaming children
were birthed from the rumbling pile, each one emerging
with a burly-armed escort.[16]

Fortunately, when children are removed from their home,
the removal is not necessarily permanent. The goal of almost
every caseworker who removes a child from the family is
someday to bring the child back to that family. The process of
bringing the child back is called reunification. According to
Judge Mary Triggiano of Milwaukee County Children's Court,
the process of reunification should begin as soon as a child

Becoming a Foster Parent

Any responsible adult can apply to be a
foster parent. Foster parents do not have
to be married and do not have to own
their own homes. Some work outside
the home, others do not. Some already
have their own children, while others
do not.

People who want to become foster
parents must first fill out an application
with their local department of children and family services. They must go
through a criminal background check
to make sure that they have never been
convicted of a crime or investigated for
child abuse. They must also show that
they can afford to meet the expenses
of a family. The state reimburses foster
families for some expenses, such as
meals. But foster families must still be
responsible for paying their own rent
and for occasional expenses such as
buying clothes and paying school fees.

is removed from a home. Social workers should immediately begin arranging visits between a child's foster family and birth family. It is important for the process to begin quickly, because most reunifications take place in the first four months after a child is placed in foster care. Most children who are placed in foster care will eventually be reunited with their families. Before reunification happens, investigators will have worked with the family to try to prevent any future acts of neglect or abuse.

CAN CHILD ABUSE
BE PREVENTED?

Twenty-three-year-old Rochanda Madry of Minneapolis, Minnesota, had five children and was overwhelmed. Most of the time she raised her children by herself with no help. One day she left her youngest daughter, who was still a baby, in the care of a friend. The friend lost control with the baby, and Madry took her daughter to the hospital with a swollen, chipped elbow joint. Because babies are unlikely to injure their own elbows, Madry's family was investigated, even though she did not injure the baby herself. Madry was later charged with neglect. She lost custody of her children temporarily and was ordered to take an eight-week parenting class. After the class she regained custody of her children.

Madry felt the class helped her enormously. She says she used to yell at her children and threaten them to get them to obey her. Now she uses time-outs to give both herself and the children time to cool off. "And when I do punish them, I let them know what the punishment is for," Madry says. Madry is also getting more help with child care now—her mother and sister stay with her children while Madry studies for the General Educational Development (GED) test to earn the equivalent of a high school diploma.

Mixed Results

Madry was not happy about being blamed for an injury that her baby received in someone else's care. She was angry when her children were removed from her care. But she was pleased with the results of the parenting class that she took. And getting extra help with child care made it possible for her to study for her

GED. The diploma would make it possible for her to get a better job and earn more money to support her family.

Child welfare experts say that Madry's case, in some ways, is typical. Parents respond much more positively to help from the community in the form of classes, child care assistance, and other resources than they do to having their children removed from their home. Research shows that when children can remain with their families, they are often safer than they are in foster care. If parents commit acts of abuse and neglect because they are overwhelmed and under too much stress, child advocates argue, it may make more sense to prevent abuse by removing parental stress and by educating parents. It costs less for the community to provide parenting classes and even financial assistance in the form of food stamps and housing subsidies than it does to go

Parenting classes can help parents properly care for their children and prevent abusive situations.

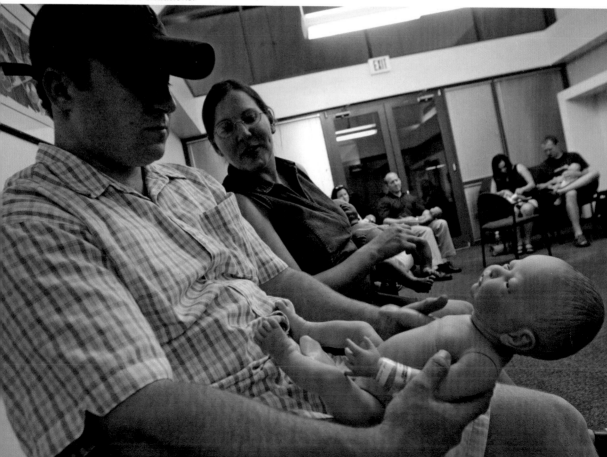

through the process of removing a child from the home, going to court, and providing foster care. And it is easier on both the parents and the children to have the state take action to support them than it is for the state to pull the family apart.

Differential Response

For these reasons, many states are choosing to offer a gentler approach to preventing child abuse than they have in the past. This gentle approach to stopping child abuse, though, coexists with the older, more adversarial model. In theory, removing children from the home is an option that should only be resorted to in extreme cases, when children are in danger. But some critics argue that investigators are too quick to remove children and that they place children in foster homes that are less safe than the children's own homes.

If a social worker determines that the risk of child abuse in the home is low to moderate, then he will work with the parents to find ways to help alleviate stress on the family without removing the child.

Some child welfare agencies are turning to a different model for investigating child abuse. Instead of investigating every report of child abuse, they classify each report based on the amount of risk to children that is involved. If a report is classified as high risk, the investigation proceeds in the traditional way. The child, parents, and caregivers are interviewed, and social workers visit the home and review the child's history. But if a case is classified as being of low to moderate risk, social workers approach it differently. Instead of formally investigating, they do an assessment. They do not make a formal determination that the report of abuse is substantiated or unsubstantiated. But they do find out what stresses the family is experiencing and offer help. Cases that are assessed this way may never make it into the juvenile court system. If the assessment were to show that children were at high risk, however, the response could be upgraded to a formal investigation.

LEARNING ABOUT LIFE

"I've been through verbal abuse, physical abuse, sexual abuse, all the abuse you can think of. . . . I ended up in three different foster homes. . . . I had one good foster family, one that taught me about morals and values. It was a pretty good family; it taught me about life." —Lou Della Casey.

Quoted in Children's Defense Fund, *The State of America's Children 2005.* www.child rensdefense.org/site/DocServer/Greenbook2005.pdf?docID=1741.

This two-tiered approach to investigating abuse is called different things in different states. Some states call it a differential response, while others call it a dual track or alternative response. The purpose of this model is to focus on keeping families together as much as possible, offering help instead of threatening to remove a child from the home. In jurisdictions where a differential response has been tried, social workers have found that parents cooperate more with child welfare agencies. An assessment does not carry the same stigma as a child abuse investigation, so parents do not feel as though their families are under attack. Another issue is that there are so many child abuse cases that the state cannot afford to investigate every one formally. Using a differential response makes it possible to prioritize the cases in which children are in the most danger.

Domestic Violence and Child Abuse

Some of the most dangerous families for children are those in which domestic violence, as well as child abuse, is occurring regularly. Research shows that domestic violence and child abuse tend to go hand-in-hand. About half of child abuse cases occur in homes in which women are being battered by their husbands or boyfriends. And about half of men who assault their wives or girlfriends also attack their children. Even those wife batterers who do not directly attack their children frequently end up hurting them accidentally when the children try to protect their mothers.

For example, Carol Johnson's partner beat her every day for four years. He caused her to have three miscarriages. She finally carried a son, Mark, to term, because her partner was in jail during the pregnancy. When Mark's father returned home from jail, he began beating Carol again. He did not attack Mark, but Mark got hurt anyway because he tried to get between his mother and father during beatings. "I knew he was going to kill us," Carol says, "but I didn't know how to leave or where to go."[17] She finally fled to another state when Mark's father was sent to jail again.

Carol was lucky that she did not lose custody of her son. Women whose partners assault them often lose custody of their children, because child welfare investigators argue that these mothers have failed to protect their children from their fathers. For example, S.N. was a thirty-one-year-old full-time college student and mother of two children. She opened her apartment door one day to find her ex-boyfriend and his two friends. Her ex-boyfriend attacked her, breaking her arm and fracturing her ribs and skull. Her nine-month-old baby was asleep in a nearby room, and her five-year-old son was at school. S.N. took her baby to a neighbor, asked her cousin to get her son from school, and then went to the hospital. The next day, she received a call

Domestic violence and child abuse go hand-in-hand as children get caught in the crossfire between their parents.

from her city's Department of Children's Services. Her children had been taken into custody and placed in foster care. The state filed a neglect case against her for exposing the children to domestic violence. It took her twenty-one days to get her children back and six months to get the neglect charges dropped.

Because domestic violence and child abuse are so closely connected, domestic violence agencies and child welfare organizations are beginning to work together to try to prevent both kinds of abuse. Battered women's shelters are beginning to be recognized by the states as safe places where women can take their children without fear of having their children taken from them. Child welfare investigators making a safety plan for a family may require batterers to go through counseling or take anger management classes. And domestic violence agencies and child welfare organizations are forming partnerships to educate the community about all the different kinds of violence that can affect families.

Education and Awareness

Organizations dedicated to the well-being of children often run campaigns to raise community awareness of child abuse and domestic violence. Domestic violence awareness campaigns are usually conducted in October, which is Domestic Violence Awareness Month. Child abuse awareness campaigns are run in April, in honor of Child Abuse Prevention Month. During these campaigns, agencies not only educate the public about the existence of family violence, but also try to encourage families to find peaceful alternatives to violence in everyday situations. For example, the Frederick County, Maryland, Partners for Child Abuse Prevention (PCAP) ran a campaign to reward parents who were patient with their children at local supermarkets. Patient parents were given a "patient parent award" and a sticker.

At the same time, PCAP ran a public awareness campaign. They put billboards all over Frederick County, emblazoned with the words "Parenting is a tough job. For help, call 662-2255." The phone number listed was the number for a parent stress line operated by the Frederick County Mental Health Association. PCAP also put messages on milk cartons, pencils, and tray liners in restaurants. Most child welfare organizations throughout the United States run campaigns like this one in April.

While most organizations run their annual child abuse awareness campaigns in April, they also try to provide support to parents year-round. The parent stress line listed in the billboard is run year-round. So are parenting classes that parents can take during a pregnancy or while their children are still young. The classes educate parents about what kinds of behaviors are normal for young children so parents do not punish age-appropriate behavior. For example, some parents do not realize until they take a parenting class that it does not make sense to spank a six-month-old for crying.

Parenting instructors also teach parents nonviolent methods for punishment, such as time-outs, so that parents have an option they can turn to when they feel that punishment is appropriate. For some parents, this is new information. Twenty-year-old Marisa Grady took a parenting class offered by the Illinois Department of Children and Family Services. "Before I took the class, I was a usual parent," says Grady. "If a child did something, I'd hit her. But now I talk to my kids more."[18] Marquita Brand had a similar experience. "I used to get frustrated a lot," she explains. "But they taught me how to sit down and talk to the children, and how to give them time-out."[19]

Nurse-Family Partnerships

Experts say that the most effective child abuse prevention programs are the ones that target mothers who are still pregnant or parents whose children are newborns. The most widespread of these programs is the Nurse-Family Partnership (NFP), which is used in 263 counties in 20 states. Colorado, Louisiana, Pennsylvania, and Oklahoma offer an NFP in each of their counties.

Home visits by nurses form the cornerstone of the NFP program. Nurses begin visiting mothers while they are still pregnant. They visit low-income, at-risk mothers who are pregnant with their first child. Because they come to a woman's home, the pregnant mother is less likely to miss her appointment than she would be if she had to go to a clinic. The nurses help mothers to make good choices about prenatal care and can offer advice about nutrition and exercise. Nurses continue to visit families until the new baby reaches the age of two. They provide parenting education. They also offer counseling and advice to mothers about life choices involving family planning, education, and finding a job.

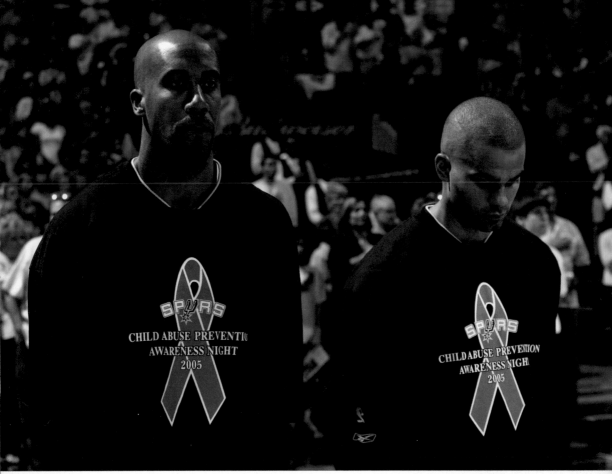

San Antonio Spurs basketball players Bruce Bowen (left) and Tony Parker wear "Child Abuse Prevention Awareness Night" shirts during the national anthem at a game against the Memphis Grizzlies on April 16, 2005.

Removal and Foster Care

Child welfare investigators, however, must also find ways to help children who have already been abused. The laws of most states now require that social workers make "reasonable efforts" to help families keep their children safe without removing the children from the family. This means that social workers must offer help. They may offer to enroll the parents in parenting classes, help parents apply for child care or housing subsidies (money from the state to help pay for child care or housing), or help parents go through the process of registering for unemployment benefits or food stamps. They may also direct parents to specific programs such as substance abuse treatment centers or clinics that provide low-cost health care. Any or all of these kinds of programs could be included in a family safety plan that child welfare investigators would prepare for a family. The plan would include a time line listing each goal and when it should be completed. For many families, these plans do help.

In many cases, though, investigators are convinced that children are in danger if they stay in their homes. Child protection workers remove approximately 15 percent of abused or neglected children from their homes. They place the children in foster care. In the United States, about eight hundred thousand children enter foster care at some point during the year. They enter family foster homes, group homes, or residential treatment centers. Not all of them stay in foster care for long. The average foster care child is ten years old, lives with a nonrelative, and has been in foster care for almost three years.

A drug addict gets treatment at a pharmacy. Social workers help addicted parents get into treatment programs with the goal of placing the children back in the home once the parents are clean.

Juvenile Court

In theory, no child should be removed from a home until parents have had a chance to tell their side of the story in court. Most of the time, though, if investigators think that children are in danger, they are able to get an emergency order authorizing the removal of the children from the home right away. Then the family is asked to appear at a hearing that occurs after the children have already been placed in foster care.

The initial hearing should include both parents and the child or children in question. If appearing in court is stressful for children, though, the judge can choose to meet with the children in chambers (the judge's office). According to Judge William Jones: "The initial hearing should establish a supportive atmosphere in which parents are treated with dignity and respect. It is a process that should focus on understanding the problems the case

Aging Out of Foster Care

There are several ways that children can leave foster care. They can be reunited with their original families. They can be placed with relatives or adopted by a new family. Many children, however, leave foster care by aging out of it. This means that they reach the age of eighteen while still living with a foster family. When children in foster care reach the age of eighteen, the state no longer acts as their guardian. They are expected to leave foster care and take care of themselves.

Children who age out of foster care, however, often are not prepared to care for themselves. Almost half of children who age out of foster care leave without having earned their high school diploma or General Educational Development (GED). Without a high school diploma or its equivalent, it is hard to get a job and earn a living. About one-third of these young people end up living below the poverty level and working in jobs that do not provide health insurance. It is especially unfortunate that they lack health insurance, because half of those who age out of the foster care system have mental illnesses. One-fifth have three or more mental illnesses. One-quarter have post-traumatic stress disorder from the abuse they have endured.

Parents who have had children removed from the home have the opportunity to plead their case before a judge in court.

presents and solving them as quickly as possible so the family can be reunited safely."[20]

In the initial hearing, the court must make decisions about how to address the family's immediate needs. The initial hearing, however, is only the first of several. There may also be an adjudication, or fact-finding, hearing. Adjudication is the process of going to court and presenting evidence at a hearing before a judge. In an adjudication hearing, the court hears evidence and tries to determine what the facts are. Finally, there is a disposition hearing, in which the court decides what kind of help the child needs and whether it is necessary to order services to be provided to the family. In some cases, the court might decide to keep the family's children in foster care while the parents resolve their own problems. For example, a judge might feel that children should be cared for by someone other than the parents if the parents are about to go through rehabilitation for a drug or alcohol problem. In other cases, the court may order that children be reunited with their parents immediately but also require the parents to go through counseling or rehabilitation.

Some juvenile courts across the country have begun to offer mediation services as an alternative to adjudication. Mediation is a gentler process for families. During mediation, families meet together with a court employee who helps the family to think through their problems and work together to devise solutions. If the family can come up with a reasonable plan, the court may approve it. If not, the family may still be able to agree about some issues, shortening the amount of time necessary to go through adjudication.

DOMESTIC VIOLENCE AND CHILD ABUSE

"There are at least 100 studies documenting the negative effects for children exposed to domestic violence." —Jeffrey Edleson, director of the Minnesota Center Against Violence and Abuse at the University of Minnesota School of Social Work.

Quoted in Stephanie Walton, "When Violence Hits Home: Responding to Domestic Violence in Families with Kids Requires a Coordinated Effort to Help the Victim and Protect the Children," *State Legislatures,* June 2003, p. 31.

When families get enough help and support early in the lives of their children, abusive situations may not arise in the first place. This is the ideal outcome. But many children do experience abuse and neglect. These children need help to make their homes safe places in which to grow up. They may also need help recovering from their experiences. With treatment for their physical and emotional injuries, children can begin to feel safe and secure again. They can leave their abuse behind them and start a new life. Many adults who were abused as children enter professions in which they help other children. These adults have come full circle. They will never be abused again, and they can help other children to regain their feelings of trust and security.

RECOVERING FROM CHILD ABUSE

"I thought I was one of the ugliest and most despicable creatures alive, inside and out," writes child abuse survivor Anna Michener.

> By the age of thirteen I was completely exhausted from merely existing in the cold, limited world my family had created for me. Although I escaped this world by sleeping as much as possible, I had constant rings under my eyes like bruises. The chronic, stress-induced stomach pain and nausea I had suffered ever since I could remember were considerably worse by the time I became a teenager, as were the headaches, dizziness, and fatigue. I was weak and sickly, always suffering from a cold or sinus infection or bronchitis. My skin was puffy and yellow, my hair dried out.[21]

Effects on Survivors

Michener's experience is typical. Physical abuse and neglect cause physical injuries and health problems such as malnutrition and anemia. But recovering from physical injuries and malnutrition is just the beginning of the healing process for most child abuse survivors. Even after a child recovers physically from abuse, emotional injuries remain. Many suffer from post-traumatic stress disorder (PTSD). Children with PTSD may suffer from unwanted memories of their abuse. Some have flashbacks during the day and nightmares at night. Others develop anxiety or depression. They may be startled easily. They may find it difficult to trust other people or to be affectionate. Some are very irritable and may be aggressive or violent themselves. Many use drugs or alcohol to try to escape from their emotions and end up with a substance abuse problem as well.

Abuse survivors who do not develop PTSD may suffer from other psychological disorders. They may suffer from low self-esteem. Many develop anxiety or depression. These survivors may even become suicidal. Children who have been abused are more likely to develop psychological disorders such as schizophrenia. They are also more likely to develop behavior problems. They may tend to argue with adults and defy authority. Many have trouble paying attention in school or following instructions. Boys, especially, tend to develop behavior problems such as fighting or destroying property.

Survivors of child abuse face a variety of crippling emotional injuries as a result of their experiences.

The Developing Brain

Psychiatrists are beginning to find, too, that the stress of abuse can affect a very young child's developing brain. Some babies who have been abused grow up unable to accept comfort from others. Preschool children who have been abused tend to have developmental delays. Developmental delays can mean, for example, that a child learns to speak later than other children or does not speak clearly. Or a delay can cause a child to take longer to learn to do physical activities that other children do easily, such as standing on one foot or holding a pencil. (There are also many medical reasons why a child might be developmentally delayed—developmental delays are not, by themselves, a sign of abuse or neglect.)

Young victims of abuse sometimes do not know how to play properly with other children or their own toys.

Psychologists have also found that preschoolers who have been abused have a harder time making full use of play materials at their preschools. They tend to touch or pound toys instead of playing with them. Some severely neglected children have never learned how to play. Instead of pretending to iron with a toy iron, for example, a preschooler who has been abused or neglected might pound the iron repetitively on the floor or put the iron in their mouths. Other children reenact their experiences of abuse in their pretend play.

RECOVERY

"I am deep into the recovery stage, but not done. Probably a few more years to go. It's hard to reverse 20 years of abuse and neglect overnight. I could not have done this, or gotten as far as I am now, without professional help. I strongly believe people have to talk to one another, and be heard, to aid in the recovery and to heal." —Holli Marshall.

Quoted in HealthyPlace, "Transcript from Online Conference with Holli Marshall and Niki Delson on 'Survivors of Sexual Abuse.'" www.healthyplace.com/COMMUNITIES/abuse/holli/interview_holli.htm.

The social skills of abused preschoolers also lag behind. These children tend to flit from one activity to another, finding it difficult to focus on one thing. They do not feel self-confident initiating a conversation with other children. They may seem hypervigilant, which means that they constantly monitor what is happening around them to make sure that the situation is safe. Children who have been physically abused or neglected sometimes act out in aggressive, disruptive ways in the classroom. They may hit or bite other children or destroy property. Children who have been sexually abused, on the other hand, more often become passive, withdrawn, and quiet.

Body Memories

Child abuse survivors often develop symptoms in their bodies that cannot be explained by a medical exam. Children may have headaches, stomachaches, or feel unusually tired all the time. Some develop diarrhea, constipation, or urinary tract infections that have no physical explanation. These symptoms are usually classified as a somatic disorder, which means that they have a psychological, not a physical, cause. A few therapists prefer to call these symptoms "body memories," because they feel that the symptoms are connected with the body's memory of having been abused. Psychotherapist Kathy Steel explains: "[Traumatized children] have problems with their body where they can't understand signals from their body and have a lot of somatic symptoms. They can't integrate their memories. They have difficulty, of course, relating with other people."[22]

Triggering the Trauma Cycle

Abuse survivors who have behavior problems tend not to have them at random times. Instead, something happens to trigger a memory of their abuse. This memory is called the trauma cycle. It is similar to a flashback. In a flashback, the survivor reexperiences the abuse, seeing the same sights, hearing the same sounds, and/or feeling the same physical sensations that happened during the abusive experience. But in the trauma cycle, survivors may simply reexperience a part of the abuse, such as the feelings and emotions that went with it. These feelings rise up in a survivor because something happens to trigger them. The trigger could be anything that reminds the survivor of the abuse—an event or even the words or tone of voice used by a teacher or a friend.

When a trigger event occurs, survivors lose their ability to think rationally. They have a fight-or-flight reaction in which their bodies are pumped full of adrenaline. The survivor's limbic system—the part of the brain responsible for basic functions such as the need for food and sleep—takes over. Bruce Perry, a doctor who specializes in pediatric brain development, explains that trigger events make children feel threatened. In response to a threat, the heart rate increases, breathing quickens, and different parts of the brain take over. Says Perry:

> The more threatened we become, the more "primitive" (or regressed) our style of thinking and behaving be-

comes. When a traumatized child is in a state of alarm (because they are thinking about the trauma, for example) they will be less capable of concentrating, they will be more anxious and they will pay more attention to "non-verbal" cues such as tone of voice, body posture and facial expressions.[23]

When this happens, survivors become hyperalert and need help to become calm again. Therapists respond when this happens by using a soft, level voice and by using neutral body language.

Memories of abuse are so vivid for child abuse survivors that they will sometimes experience the abuse again in a flashback.

Flashbacks

Survivors of child abuse often experience flashbacks, even years after the abuse is over. A flashback is a memory that is so intense that it feels as though the survivor is reliving the experience. Some flashbacks are so real that the person experiencing them sees, hears, and feels the abuse happening all over again. Other flashbacks are more fragmentary—a survivor might remember just an image, or a feeling, that dates back to the abuse. Either way, flashbacks can be very stressful and even terrifying.

Survivors who experience flashbacks often find that counseling and psychotherapy can be very helpful. During a flashback, it can help to open one's eyes and look around, making sure to notice things that make one feel safe. Some survivors carry a special rock or other object in a pocket and hold the object during a flashback as a way of trying to feel more secure. It can also help to notice what triggers a flashback—what words, images, smells, or sounds cause those memories to return.

For many survivors, authority figures can trigger the trauma cycle to recur. In their birth families, these survivors may have been subjected to parents or caregivers who insisted on obedience and who also abused them. These survivors feel more secure if they are in an environment where they have more choices about what they do and do not want to do next. When they are subjected to authority, such as the authority of a classroom teacher, these children may appear to have behavior problems. Girls may seem not to be paying attention. Boys may seem hyperactive. Both may have difficulty doing math problems, for example, when they are called to the front of the classroom. It is hard to do schoolwork after something has triggered a memory of abuse, because the memory brings up a compelling array of emotions. Therapists respond to this kind of situation by trying to give children more control. Perry explains, "If a child is given some choice or some element of control in an activity or in an interaction with an adult, they will feel more safe, comfortable and will be able to feel, think and act in a more 'mature' fashion."[24]

Is It Possible to Recover?

When Illinois acupuncturist Nancy Floy was four years old, her father worked at a day care center. He and the other workers at the day care center joined a religious cult and began to ritually abuse all of the children at the day care center. (Ritual abuse is an extremely cruel form of abuse in which the abusers use torture to try to brainwash their victims, using the abuse to try to force victims to accept a religion or an ideology.) Floy's father raped her.

Leeza Gibbons interviews a man whose father set him on fire when he was six years old. The man, known by his first name, "Dave," talked about his physical and emotional recovery from his child abuse with Gibbons on her television show in 1996.

Eventually, some of the older girls at the day care center told their parents what was happening. The workers, including Floy's father, were arrested and went on trial. All the children from the day care center testified at the trial. Some of the workers were sent to mental hospitals, but Floy's father went to prison. Her mother had a nervous breakdown and was unable to continue to care for her. Floy was safe, for the moment, but she needed a home. She was placed in a group home, an institution that provided medical care for her physical injuries and psychotherapy for her emotional trauma. At age five, Floy says, she began to heal. Eventually, she was released to kinship care—she moved in with her grandmother, who helped her to continue the process of healing.

MOTHERS AND HEALING

"If it is a family member, an incestuous relationship, then the mother is the key to the healing. Research clearly demonstrates that children who have supportive mothers who acknowledge the molestation experience and clearly hold the perpetrator accountable, will heal faster." —Niki Delson.

Quoted in HealthyPlace, "Transcript from Online Conference with Holli Marshall and Niki Delson on 'Survivors of Sexual Abuse.'" www.healthyplace.com/COMMUNITIES/abuse/holli/interview_holli.htm.

Coming Full Circle

As an adult, Floy came full circle. She began to work with women who had been abused, running a battered women's shelter. Then she began to study Chinese medicine and became an acupuncturist. Finally, she opened a center for healing—the Heartwood Center for Body, Mind, and Spirit.

Holli Marshall, like Nancy Floy, was severely abused at a very young age. She was raped at age five and continued to be abused and raped over a period of several years. Her mother was mentally ill and neglected her. "She couldn't take care of me, much less herself," says Marshall. "I'd go days without food, having my clothes changed, and without being held or nurtured." Like other children who have survived abuse, Marshall developed physical symptoms and post-traumatic stress disorder. She says: "It's as if I've been through the Vietnam war and I experienced all the symptoms of PTSD. For instance, I had nightmares, flashbacks, hot and cold sweats, anorexia, abdominal distress, stomach pain, migraines and I'm a very nervous and anxious person."[25]

Like Floy, Marshall has come full circle. She is disabled because of the abuse that she experienced and will be for the rest of her life. After many years of therapy, she decided to start her own Web site. She works to improve public awareness about child abuse and directs survivors to resources that can help them in their recovery.

A Safe Place

Floy's and Marshall's stories show that it is possible for an abused child to come full circle. It is possible not only to recover, but to help others to recover, too. The journey toward recovery, however, can take many years. The first step for Floy and Marshall, and for most child abuse survivors, was to have a safe place to heal physically and to begin psychotherapy. Dale Latimer, a high school teacher who works with emotionally disturbed children, explains why feeling safe is so important. "The first thing you have to provide for them is a safe, comfortable environment," he says. "Number one, they need to develop a feeling of trust and comfort and security. And it needs to go for a long period of time—it's got to be something that they can count on day in and day out."[26]

Former foster child Robert Kendall agrees. He says:

> Deep down, kids all want the same stuff. They all want to be loved, they all want a family. And they all want to know why they didn't have a family and they weren't loved. They're trying to figure out why everything happened to them and can it ever be okay . . . so that they can say to themselves, "It will be okay, and I can relax, and these people aren't going to hurt me."[27]

Two girls find a safe haven at the World Vision Children of War Rehabilitation Center after escaping from the Lord's Resistance Army in Uganda. The rebel group has kidnapped thousands of children, forcing them into combat and sexual slavery during an eighteen-year-long civil war in that country.

Not until children feel safe and secure can they really begin the process of healing. Once Floy had a safe place to live, she began her therapy. The institution where she lived offered psychotherapy, art therapy, and play therapy. Psychotherapy is sometimes called talk therapy or counseling. It means taking time to talk about the abuse and its continuing effects. Psychotherapists try to help children understand that what happened to them was not their fault and to find ways to process and release their memories of abuse. Therapists working with young children often use art therapy and play therapy as well. Art therapy means using creative processes, such as music, dance, movement, drama, drawing, painting, and poetry, to work through negative memories and emotions. Play therapy is a type of therapy aimed at very young children who may have trouble expressing their feelings in words. They can use dolls and toys to help them to tell a therapist about what happened to them and how they feel about it.

Like Floy, Marshall began therapy at an early age. She says:

> I've been through "talk" therapy, doing some hypnosis, meditation, relaxation and breathing techniques. I've also been put on medications, Prozac, Klonopin, Vistoril. All have been very helpful combined together. I also have a wonderful psychologist who specializes in working with those with post-traumatic stress disorder. The therapy, the healing process, creates safety about you and teaches you how to create a support system. You learn how to cope, nurture yourself, build self-esteem and confidence, build better relationships and boundaries within those relationships. You learn how to live with the feeling of "impending doom."[28]

As they talk with children about abuse, therapists try to focus on the positive—the fact that children survived and are still

Psychotherapy

Many survivors of abuse find that psychotherapy helps them to reduce or manage their symptoms, such as depression, anxiety, flashbacks, and attention disorders. To get psychotherapy, survivors must go to a licensed psychologist—a doctor who has a PhD and has been licensed by the state to treat mental disorders. Not all survivors feel they need psychotherapy. But those who sometimes think of committing suicide or who consider hurting themselves or others usually can benefit from seeing a psychologist or psychiatrist.

Psychotherapy is also helpful for survivors who have trouble functioning in everyday life because of their symptoms. For example, some survivors have trouble concentrating in school or at work because of their feelings of anxiety. Others have flashbacks that interfere with their ability to function normally during the day.

Psychotherapy is often called talk therapy because it consists mostly of talking to a therapist. However, psychiatrists also have the option to prescribe medication if they feel their patients need it.

here to tell the tale of what happened. "One of the first things you need to ask," says psychiatrist Bessel van der Kolk, "is, how did you survive this?" He goes on: "This is amazing that you're still here. It's amazing that you still have the guts to go on with your life. What is allowing you to function? What are you good at? What gives you comfort?"[29]

Meditation

For Floy, one of the things that gave her the most comfort was the practice of meditation. When she left her institutional home, she entered kinship care—she lived with her grandmother. Her grandmother, a Buddhist, taught her to meditate. Although Floy's meditation practice came from her grandmother's practice

Physical activity, such as karate, can help child abuse survivors feel good about themselves.

of Buddhism, she encourages abuse survivors of any religious tradition to add meditation to their daily routine. Meditation is the practice of sitting quietly and being mindful. Although sitting mindfully and paying attention may not sound like a powerful experience, Floy explains that meditation can give survivors a safe way to be with themselves. "Then," she says, "you have that to draw on for the rest of your life."[30]

Another type of meditation that helps many survivors is moving meditation through the practice of martial arts or yoga. In fact, says Floy, any physical practice that a survivor enjoys, whether it be learning karate, doing yoga, or trying out for a sport at school, can help in the healing process. Enjoyable physical activities give survivors good body memories to balance the negative memories of their traumatic experiences. The good memories, unfortunately, do not overwrite the bad ones. But they provide a safe memory that survivors can try to go back to when they find themselves caught up in a flashback.

Finding a Healer

Floy believes that it is important for survivors to find a healer with whom they can connect. This healer could be a massage therapist, doctor, yoga teacher, coach, or meditation teacher. Whoever it is, it should be someone who has faith in the survivor's ability to heal and move beyond the abuse. Massage therapy can be especially good for survivors because it gives them a chance to experience another person touching their bodies in a positive, loving way. Yoga, says Floy, is also very helpful, because it helps the body to release tension that may have been stored in a survivor's body since the abuse occurred. Marshall agrees. For her, being on her school track team helped her to begin to recover. She also found that listening to music was very helpful.

For all abuse survivors, the key to recovery is to develop a healthy sense of self-esteem and self-confidence. "I believe that we are all born perfect," says Floy, "with basic goodness. Abuse is like film on a windshield. We just need to scrape it away, or wait for the clouds to clear."[31] Then, she says, a survivor's basic goodness—his or her inner beauty—can shine through.

Introduction: More than a Million Children

1. Houghton Mifflin, *The American Heritage Dictionary of the English Language*, 4th ed. Boston: Houghton Mifflin, 2000, p. 839.

2. Richard Pelzer, *A Brother's Journey: Surviving a Childhood of Abuse.* New York: Warner, 2005, p. 1.

Chapter 1: How Serious Is Child Abuse in the United States?

3. Gavin de Becker, *Protecting the Gift: Keeping Children and Teenagers Safe (and Parents Sane).* New York: Dial, 1999, p. 22.

4. Marc Parent, *Turning Stones: My Days and Nights with Children at Risk.* New York: Harcourt Brace, 1996, p. 304.

5. Parent, *Turning Stones*, pp. 175–76.

6. Quoted in Karen Gardner, "April Is Child Abuse Prevention Month: Patient Parents Get Rewards in This Promotion," *Frederick News-Post*, April 9, 1993, p. B-5.

7. J. Robert Shull, "Emotional and Psychological Child Abuse: Notes on Discourse, History, and Change," *Stanford Law Review*, July 1, 1999, p. 1665.

8. James Garbarino, Edna Guttman, and Janis Wilson Seeley, *The Psychologically Battered Child: Strategies for Identification, Assessment and Intervention.* San Francisco: Jossey-Bass, 1986, p. 12.

Chapter 2: When Does Child Abuse Happen?

9. Quoted in Chris Berdik, "Poor Little Rich Kids," *Boston Magazine*, December 2003. www.bostonmagazine.com/articles/poor_little_rich_kids.

10. Parent, *Turning Stones*, p. 97.

11. Quoted in Dan Benson, "West Bend Man Charged with Abuse: 2-Month-Old Girl Put on Life Support," *Milwaukee Journal Sentinel*, August 14, 2008, p. B1.

12. Quoted in Benson, "West Bend Man Charged with Abuse," p. B1.

Chapter 3: How Is Child Abuse Investigated?

13. Quoted in Cavalcade Productions, "Trauma and Dissociation in Children." www.cavalcadeproductions.com/traumaand dissociation.html.

14. Dave Pelzer, *A Child Called "It": One Child's Courage to Survive*. Deerfield Beach, FL: Health Communications, 1995, pp. 9–10.

15. Parent, *Turning Stones*, pp. 83–84.

16. Parent, *Turning Stones*, pp. 284–85.

Chapter 4: Can Child Abuse Be Prevented?

17. Quoted in Stephanie Walton, "When Violence Hits Home: Responding to Domestic Violence in Families with Kids Requires a Coordinated Effort to Help the Victim and Protect the Children," *State Legislatures*, June 2003, p. 31.

18. Quoted in Lisa Jones, "Why Are We Beating Our Children? An Upsurge in Child Abuse Cases Raises New Questions," *Ebony*, March 1993, p. 80.

19. Quoted in Jones, "Why Are We Beating Our Children?" p. 80.

20. William Jones, *Working with the Courts in Child Protection*. U.S. Department of Health and Human Services, 2006. www.childwelfare.gov/pubs/usermanuals/courts/courts .pdf.

Chapter 5: Recovering from Child Abuse

21. Anna Michener, *Becoming Anna: The Autobiography of a Sixteen-Year-Old*. Chicago: University of Chicago Press, 1998, p. 11.

22. Quoted in Cavalcade Productions, "Trauma and Dissociation in Children."

23. Bruce Perry, "Principles of Working with Traumatized Children," Scholastic. http://teacher.scholastic.com/professional/bruceperry/working_children.htm.

24. Perry, "Principles of Working with Traumatized Children."

25. Quoted in HealthyPlace, "Transcript from Online Conference with Holli Marshall and Niki Delson on 'Survivors of Sexual Abuse.'" www.healthyplace.com/COMMUNITIES/abuse/holli/interview_holli.htm.

26. Quoted in Cavalcade Productions, "The Traumatized Child."

27. Quoted in Cavalcade Productions, "The Traumatized Child."

28. Quoted in HealthyPlace, "Transcript from Online Conference with Holli Marshall and Niki Delson on 'Survivors of Sexual Abuse.'"

29. Quoted in Cavalcade Productions, "Severe Early Trauma." Video series. www.cavalcadeproductions.com/childhood-trauma.html.

30. Nancy Floy, interview with the author, Evanston, IL, August 2008.

31. Floy interview.

GLOSSARY

adjudication: The process of going to court and presenting evidence at hearings before a judge.

differential response: A response to child abuse that involves making an informal assessment and safety plan rather than starting a formal investigation into a family.

domestic violence: Violence that occurs between two people who form a romantic couple, such as a husband and wife, boyfriend and girlfriend, or a gay or lesbian couple.

emotional abuse: Abuse that causes a psychological injury.

flashbacks: Intense memories of abuse that make the survivor feel as if he or she is reliving the experience.

foster care: Temporary or permanent out-of-home care for a child.

homicide: A death caused by another person, such as when a child dies of injuries incurred during an abusive incident.

kinship care: Foster care in which a child's relative acts as the foster parent.

mandated reporter: A person whose job requires reporting any suspected child abuse.

mediation: An alternative to adjudication in which families get involved in the process of forming a safety plan.

neglect: Depriving a child of food, clothing, shelter, medical care, or supervision.

perpetrator: A term used by law enforcement officials to describe the person who committed a crime.

physical abuse: Any nonaccidental injury to a child.

reunification: Returning a child to his or her own family after the child has been in foster care.

shaken baby syndrome: Injuries caused when a baby is shaken.

substantiated: Documented with evidence.

unsubstantiated: Unable to be documented with evidence.

DISCUSSION QUESTIONS

Chapter 1: How Serious Is Child Abuse in the United States?

1. What does the author say is the difference between physical abuse and neglect?

2. Why is it difficult to collect accurate statistics about child abuse?

3. How do doctors detect physical abuse?

Chapter 2: When Does Child Abuse Happen?

1. Describe the average perpetrator of child abuse.

2. Describe the demographic category of the children who are most at risk for child abuse. Then explain why these children are at so much risk.

3. How do child fatalities occur? Describe some typical cases.

Chapter 3: How Is Child Abuse Investigated?

1. Name some types of mandated reporters.

2. What steps do investigators go through as they investigate a case of child abuse?

3. What is the difference between a substantiated and an unsubstantiated case of child abuse?

Chapter 4: Can Child Abuse Be Prevented?

1. What does the author say that child welfare agencies do in order to prevent child abuse?

2. What is the difference between a differential response and a traditional child abuse investigation?

3. How is domestic violence connected with child abuse?

Chapter 5: Recovering from Child Abuse

1. How do child abuse and neglect affect survivors?

2. How does post-traumatic stress disorder (PTSD) affect survivors?

3. Name some of the things a survivor would probably have to do in order to begin the process of recovery from child abuse and neglect.

ORGANIZATIONS TO CONTACT

Child Welfare League of America (CWLA)
2345 Crystal Dr., Ste. 250
Arlington, VA 22202
Phone: (703) 412-2400
Fax: (703) 412-2401
Web site: www.cwla.org

CWLA trains and educates child welfare workers and tries to increase awareness about child abuse among the public. It produces publications related to child abuse, and offers conferences and classes.

Childhelp
15757 N. Seventy-eighth St.
Scottsdale, AZ 85260
Phone: (480) 922-8212
Fax: (480) 922-7061
Hotline: (800) 422-4453
Web site: www.childhelp.org

Childhelp runs residential treatment programs and group homes for abused children and offers advocacy services for children. It also produces educational materials to increase public awareness about child abuse. Childhelp's child abuse hotline is staffed seven days a week, twenty-four hours a day, and receives phone calls from all fifty U.S. states, Canada, the U.S. Virgin Islands, Puerto Rico, and Guam.

Children's Defense Fund
25 E St. NW
Washington, DC 20001
Phone: (202) 628-8787
Web site: www.childrensdefense.org

The Children's Defense Fund lobbies state legislatures and Congress about laws that affect children. It also works to educate the public and increase awareness about issues that disproportionately affect children, such as abuse and poverty. Child abuse is only one of several areas that the CDF focuses on.

International Child Abuse Network (Yes ICAN)
7657 Winnetka Ave., PMB 155
Canoga Park, CA 91306-2677
Phone: (888) 224-4226 (NOT A CRISIS LINE)
Fax: (818) 716-0658
Web site: www.yesican.org/index.html

Yes ICAN is an organization dedicated to providing information and increasing awareness about child abuse internationally. The Web site includes basic information about child abuse, links to news stories, and book recommendations for survivors and for concerned friends and family members.

National Council on Child Abuse and Family Violence (NCCAFV)
1025 Connecticut Ave. NW, Ste. 1000
Washington, DC 20036
Phone: (202) 429-6695
Fax: (202) 521-3479
Hotline: (800) 799-7233 or (800) 787-3244
Web site: www.nccafv.org

NCCAFV's mission is to connect community members, professionals, and volunteers to prevent domestic violence and child abuse. It staffs a hotline providing referrals to organizations that can help survivors to find a safe place to stay and to get legal help.

FOR MORE INFORMATION

Books

Patti Feuereisen, *Invisible Girls: The Truth About Sexual Abuse*. Seal Press, 2005. Written by a therapist for teenagers, this book includes many personal stories of abuse and healing.

Kathy Harrison, *Another Place at the Table*. Los Angeles: Tarcher, 2004. Harrison tells her personal story of opening her home to foster children. She explains how the foster care system works and talks about the challenges many foster children face.

Betsy Krebs and Paul Pitcoff, *Beyond the Foster Care System: The Future for Teens*. Piscataway, NJ: Rutgers University Press, 2006. Krebs and Pitcoff argue that the foster care system does not serve teens well and does not adequately prepare them to be independent as adults. They argue that teens in foster care need more help to prepare them for adulthood.

M. Foster Olive, *Child Abuse and Stress Disorders*. New York: Chelsea House, 2006. Covers the role of child abuse in contributing to stress disorders such as anxiety, depression, and post-traumatic stress disorder.

Murray Straus, Richard Gelles, and Suzanne Steinmetz, *Behind Closed Doors: Violence in the American Family*. Piscataway, NJ: Transaction, 2006. This book provides the most recent version of Straus and Gelles's seminal research into family violence, along with their conclusions and recommendations for policy changes.

Web Sites

Children's Defense Fund (www.childrensdefense.org/site/Page Server). Contains many publications full of statistical information about children, poverty, and abuse and neglect, among other topics.

Definitions of Child Abuse and Neglect: Summary of State Laws, Child Welfare Information Gateway (www.childwel fare.gov/systemwide/laws_policies/statutes/defineall.pdf). Summarizes state laws on abuse and neglect. Also gives a state-by-state breakdown of laws related to abuse and neglect. A good source to start with if the laws for a particular state are needed. The Child Welfare Information Gateway has other helpful resources as well, including statistics on child abuse and links to articles about the process of investigation.

Healing Resources.info: Preventing and Healing Stress-Related Problems (www.traumaresources.org). This site is sponsored by the Santa Barbara Graduate Institute Center for Clinical Studies and Research and the L.A. County Early Identification and Intervention Group. It includes information about the process of healing from child trauma and articles and video footage.

National Domestic Violence Hotline (www.ndvh.org). The Web site of the National Domestic Violence Hotline (800-799-7233). Includes articles about the connection between domestic violence and child abuse, and statistics concerning the prevalence of domestic violence in the United States.

National Runaway Switchboard (www.nrscrisisline.org). Includes statistics and information about runaway and throw-away children, as well as links to resources for children who are in a crisis. The National Runaway Switchboard also runs a hotline (800-786-2929).

INDEX

PICTURE CREDITS

Cover image: © Christine Schneider/zefa/Corbis

Maury Aaseng, 18, 36

AP Images, 11, 13, 23, 37, 59, 79

© B.A.E., Inc./Alamy, 50

© Roger Bamber/Alamy, 77

© Robin Beckham/Alamy, 31

Chris Birck/NBAE via Getty Images, 66

© Bubbles Photolibrary/Alamy, 63, 73

© David Hoffman Photo Library/Alamy, 67

Marco Di Lauro/Getty Images, 82

© Elmtree Images/Alamy, 69

© Andrew Fox/Alamy, 84

Steve Kagan/Time Life Pictures/Getty Images, 44, 47

© Brenda Ann Kenneally/Corbis, 53

© Medical-on-Line/Alamy, 34

© Abraham Menashe/Alamy, 28, 60

© Mira/Alamy, 15

© Gabe Palmer/Alamy, 42

© Gary Roebuck/Alamy, 74

SuperStock/Jupiterimages, 8

© Ian Thraves/Alamy, 27

© vario images GMbH & Co.KG/Alamy, 20

Scott G. Winterton/Deseret Morning News/Getty Images, 54

ABOUT THE AUTHOR

Bonnie Juettner is a writer and editor of children's reference books and educational videos. As a mother of two, she has a special interest in children's issues. She first began learning about abuse as an employee of Chicago Abused Women Coalition and Greenhouse Shelter. She is also very interested in the connection between violence, self-defense, and peace. She is a former board member of Chimera Self Defense for Women and a black-belt student of Thousand Waves Martial Arts and Self-Defense Center in Chicago.